OLAUDAH EQUIANO

Sold as a Slave

GREAT
JOURNEYS

PENGUIN BOOKS

Published by the Penguin Group
Penguin Books Ltd, 80 Strand, London WC2R 0RL, England
Penguin Group (USA) Inc., 375 Hudson Street, New York, New York 10014, USA
Penguin Group (Canada), 90 Eglinton Avenue East, Suite 700, Toronto, Ontario, Canada M4P 2Y3
(a division of Pearson Penguin Canada Inc.)
Penguin Ireland, 25 St Stephen's Green, Dublin 2, Ireland (a division of Penguin Books Ltd)
Penguin Group (Australia), 250 Camberwell Road, Camberwell, Victoria 3124, Australia
(a division of Pearson Australia Group Pty Ltd)
Penguin Books India Pvt Ltd, 11 Community Centre, Panchsheel Park, New Delhi – 110 017, India
Penguin Group (NZ), 67 Apollo Drive, Mairangi Bay, Auckland 1310, New Zealand
(a division of Pearson New Zealand Ltd)
Penguin Books (South Africa) (Pty) Ltd, 24 Sturdee Avenue, Rosebank, Johannesburg 2196, South Africa

Penguin Books Ltd, Registered Offices: 80 Strand, London WC2R 0RL, England

www.penguin.com

The Interesting Narrative of the Life of Olaudah Equiano first published 1789
This extract published in Penguin Books 2007

1

Inside-cover maps by Jeff Edwards

Typeset by Rowland Phototypesetting Ltd, Bury St Edmunds, Suffolk
Printed in England by Clays Ltd, St Ives plc

ISBN: 978-0-141-02544-5

Contents

Olaudah Equiano (*c.* 1745–97) led an extraordinarily complex and adventurous life and his autobiography, *The Interesting Narrative* (1789), is one of the great documents on the nature of slavery. As these extracts show, however, it is also much more than that and is at least as interesting about life in the Royal Navy, Equiano having served in the Seven Years' War, both in North America and in Europe.

It seems almost certain that the famous opening section, dealing with life in Benin, is a fabrication, albeit a fabrication based on good sources. Equiano was probably born in South Carolina rather than Benin. However, the narrative that follows of slavery, life in the Navy and then the terrible treachery that returned him to slavery are absolutely authentic. Ultimately Equiano settled in England, became a celebrity through the publication of *The Interesting Narrative*, married, had two children and died there.

1. No Beasts of Husbandry

That part of Africa, known by the name of Guinea, to which the trade for slaves is carried on, extends along the coast above 3400 miles, from Senegal to Angola, and includes a variety of kingdoms. Of these the most considerable is the kingdom of Benin, both as to extent and wealth, the richness and cultivation of the soil, the power of its king, and the number and warlike disposition of the inhabitants. It is situated nearly under the line and extends along the coast about 170 miles, but runs back into the interior part of Africa to a distance hitherto I believe unexplored by any traveller; and seems only terminated at length by the empire of Abyssinia, near 1500 miles from its beginning. This kingdom is divided into many provinces or districts: in one of the most remote and fertile of which [, called Eboe,] I was born, in the year 1745, in a charming fruitful vale, named Essaka. The distance of this province from the capital of Benin and the sea coast must be very considerable; for I had never heard of white men or Europeans, nor of the sea; and our subjection to the king of Benin was little more than nominal; for every transaction of the government, as far as my slender observation extended, was conducted by the chiefs or elders of the place. The manners and government of a people who have little commerce with other

Olaudah Equiano

countries are generally very simple; and the history of what passes in one family or village may serve as a specimen of the whole nation. My father was one of those elders or chiefs I have spoken of, and was styled Embrenché; a term, as I remember, importing the highest distinction, and signifying in our language a mark of grandeur. This mark is conferred on the person entitled to it, by cutting the skin across at the top of the forehead, and drawing it down to the eye-brows; and, while it is in this situation, applying a warm hand, and rubbing it until it shrinks up into a thick *weal* across the lower part of the forehead. Most of the judges and senators were thus marked; my father had long borne it: I had seen it conferred on one of my brothers, and I was also *destined* to receive it by my parents. Those Embrenché, or chief men, decided disputes and punished crimes; for which purpose they always assembled together. The proceedings were generally short; and in most cases the law of retaliation prevailed. I remember a man was brought before my father, and the other judges, for kidnapping a boy; and, although he was the son of a chief or senator, he was condemned to make recompense by a man or woman slave. Adultery, however, was sometimes punished with slavery or death; a punishment which I believe is inflicted on it throughout most of the nations of Africa: so sacred among them is the honour of the marriage bed, and so jealous are they of the fidelity of their wives. Of this I recollect an instance. – A woman was convicted before the judges of adultery, and delivered over, as the custom was, to her husband to be punished.

Accordingly he determined to put her to death: but it being found, just before her execution, that she had an infant at her breast; and no woman being prevailed on to perform the part of a nurse, she was spared on account of the child. The men, however, do not preserve the same constancy to their wives, which they expect from them; for they indulge in a plurality, though seldom in more than two. Their mode of marriage is thus: – both parties are usually betrothed when young by their parents (though I have known the males to betroth themselves). On this occasion a feast is prepared, and the bride and bridegroom stand up in the midst of all their friends, who are assembled for the purpose, while he declares she is thenceforth to be looked upon as his wife, and that no other person is to pay any addresses to her. This is also immediately proclaimed in the vicinity, on which the bride retires from the assembly. Some time after, she is brought home to her husband, and then another feast is made, to which the relations of both parties are invited: her parents then deliver her to the bridegroom, accompanied with a number of blessings, and at the same time they tie round her waist a cotton string of the thickness of a goose-quill, which none but married women are permitted to wear: she is now considered as completely his wife; and at this time the dowry is given to the new married pair, which generally consists of portions of land, slaves, and cattle, household goods, and implements of husbandry. These are offered by the friends of both parties; besides which the parents of the bridegroom present gifts to those of the bride, whose property she is looked upon before marriage; but after it she is esteemed the sole property of her husband. The ceremony being now ended, the festival begins, which is celebrated with bonfires, and loud acclamations of joy, accompanied with music and dancing.

We are almost a nation of dancers, musicians, and poets. Thus every great event, such as a triumphant return from battle, or other cause of public rejoicing, is celebrated in public dances, which are accompanied with songs and music suited to the occasion. The assembly is separated into four divisions, which dance either apart or in succession, and each with a character peculiar to itself. The first division contains the married men, who in their dances frequently exhibit feats of arms, and the representation of a battle. To these succeed the married women, who dance in the second division. The young men occupy the third; and the maidens the fourth. Each represents some interesting scene of real life, such as a great achievement, domestic employment, a pathetic story, or some rural sport; and as the subject is generally founded on some recent event, it is therefore ever new. This gives our dances a spirit and variety which I have scarcely seen elsewhere. We have many musical instruments, particularly drums of different kinds, a piece of music which resembles a guitar, and another much like a stickado. These last are chiefly used by betrothed virgins, who play on them on all grand festivals.

As our manners are simple, our luxuries are few. The dress of both sexes is nearly the same. It generally consists of a long piece of calico, or muslin, wrapped loosely round the body, somewhat in the form of a Highland plaid. This is usually dyed blue, which is our favourite colour. It is extracted from a berry, and is brighter and richer than any I have seen in Europe. Besides this, our women of distinction wear golden ornaments, which they dispose with some profusion on their arms and legs. When our women are not employed with the men in tillage, their usual occupation is spinning and weaving cotton, which they afterwards dye, and make into garments. They also manufacture earthen vessels, of which we have many kinds. Among the rest tobacco pipes, made after the same fashion, and used in the same manner, as those in Turkey.

Our manner of living is entirely plain; for as yet the natives are unacquainted with those refinements in cookery which debauch the taste: bullocks, goats, and poultry supply the greatest part of their food. These constitute likewise the principal wealth of the country, and the chief articles of its commerce. The flesh is usually stewed in a pan. To make it savory, we sometimes use also pepper, and other spices, and we have salt made of wood ashes. Our vegetables are mostly plantains, eadas, yams, beans, and Indian corn. The head of the family usually eats alone; his wives and slaves have also their separate tables. Before we taste food, we always wash our hands: indeed our cleanliness on all occasions is extreme; but on this it is an indispensable ceremony. After washing, libation is made, by pouring out a small portion of the drink on the floor, and tossing a small quantity of the food in a certain place, for the spirits of departed relations, which the natives suppose to preside over their conduct, and guard them from evil. They are totally unacquainted with strong or spirituous liquours; and their principal beverage is palm wine. This is got from a tree of that name, by tapping it at the top, and fastening a large gourd to it; and sometimes one tree will yield three or four gallons in a night. When just drawn it is of a most delicious sweetness; but in a few days it acquires a tartish and more spirituous flavour: though I never saw any one intoxicated by it. The same tree also produces nuts and oil. Our principal luxury is in perfumes; one sort of these is an odoriferous wood of delicious fragrance: the other a kind of earth; a small portion of which thrown into the fire diffuses a most powerful odour. We beat this wood into powder, and mix it with palm-oil; with which both men and women perfume themselves.

In our buildings we study convenience rather than ornament. Each master of a family has a large square piece of ground, surrounded with a moat or fence, or enclosed with a wall made of red earth tempered, which, when dry, is as hard as brick. Within this are his houses to accommodate his family and slaves; which, if numerous, frequently present the appearance of a village. In the middle stands the principal building, appropriated to the sole use of the master, and consisting of two apartments; in one of which he sits in the day with his family, the other is left apart for the reception of his friends. He has besides these a distinct apartment in which he sleeps, together with his male children. On each side are the apartments of his wives, who have also their separate day and night houses. The habitations of the slaves and their families are distributed throughout the rest of the enclosure. These houses never exceed one storey in height; they are always built of wood, or stakes driven into the ground, crossed with wattles, and neatly plastered within, and without. The roof is thatched with reeds. Our day-houses are left open at the sides; but those in which we sleep are always covered, and plastered in the inside, with a composition mixed with cow-dung, to keep off the different insects which annoy us during the night. The walls and floors also of these are generally covered with mats. Our beds consist of a platform, raised three or four feet from the ground, on which are laid skins, and different parts of a spungy tree called plaintain. Our covering is calico or muslin, the same as our dress. The usual seats are a few logs of wood; but we have benches, which are generally perfumed, to accommo-date strangers; these compose the greater part of our household furniture. Houses so constructed and fur-nished require but little skill to erect them. Every man is a sufficient architect for the purpose. The whole neighbourhood afford their unanimous assistance in building them, and, in return, receive and expect no other recompense than a feast.

As we live in a country where nature is prodigal of her favours, our wants are few and easily supplied; of course we have few manufactures. They consist for the most part of calicoes, earthen ware, ornaments, and instruments of war and husbandry. But these make no part of our commerce, the principal articles of which, as I have observed, are provisions. In such a state money is of little use; however we have some small pieces of coin, if I may call them such. They are made something like an anchor; but I do not remember either their value or denomination. We have also markets, at which I have been frequently with my mother. These are sometimes visited by stout, mahogany-coloured men from the south west of us: we call them *Oye-Eboe*, which term signifies red men living at a distance. They generally bring us firearms, gun-powder, hats, beads, and dried fish. The last we esteemed a great rarity, as our waters were only brooks and springs. These articles they barter with us for odoriferous woods and earth, and our salt of wood-ashes. They always carry slaves through our land; but the strictest account is exacted of their manner of procuring them before they are suffered to pass. Sometimes indeed we sold slaves to them, but they were only prisoners of war, or such among us as had been convicted of kidnapping, or adultery, and some other crimes which we esteemed heinous. This practice of kidnapping induces me to think, that, notwithstanding all our strictness, their principal business among us was to trepan our people. I remember too they carried great sacks along with them, which, not long after, I had an opportunity of fatally seeing applied to that infamous purpose.

Our land is uncommonly rich and fruitful, and produces all kinds of vegetables in great abundance. We have plenty of Indian corn, and vast quantities of cotton and tobacco. Our pine apples grow without culture; they are about the size of the largest sugar-loaf, and finely flavoured. We have also spices of different kinds, particularly pepper; and a variety of delicious fruits which I have never seen in Europe; together with gums of various kinds, and honey in abundance. All our industry is exerted to improve those blessings of nature. Agriculture is our chief employment; and every one, even the children and women, are engaged in it. Thus we are all habituated to labour from our earliest years. Every one contributes something to the common stock; and as we are unacquainted with idleness, we have no beggars. The benefits of such a mode of living are obvious. The West-India planters prefer the slaves of Benin or Eboe to those of any other part of Guinea, for their hardiness, intelligence, integrity, and zeal. Those benefits are felt by us in the general healthiness of the people, and in their vigour and activity; I might have added too in their comeliness. Deformity is indeed unknown amongst us, I mean that of shape. Numbers of the natives of Eboe now in London might be brought in support of this assertion; for, in regard to complexion, ideas of beauty are wholly relative. I remember while in Africa to have seen three negro children, who were tawny, and another quite white, who were universally regarded by myself and the natives in general, as far as related to their complexions, as deformed. Our women too were, in my eyes at least, uncommonly graceful, alert, and modest to a degree of bashfulness; nor do I remember to have ever heard of an instance of incontinence amongst them before marriage. They are also remarkably cheerful. Indeed cheerfulness and affability are two of the leading characteristics of our nation.

Our tillage is exercised in a large plain or common, some hours walk from our dwellings, and all the neighbours resort thither in a body. They use no beasts of husbandry; and their only instruments are hoes, axes, shovels, and beaks, or pointed iron to dig with. Sometimes we are visited by locusts, which come in large clouds, so as to darken the air, and destroy our harvest. This however happens rarely, but when it does, a famine is produced by it. I remember an instance or two wherein this happened. This common is oftimes the theatre of war; and therefore when our people go out to till their land, they not only go in a body, but generally take their arms with them, for fear of a surprise; and when they apprehend an invasion they guard the avenues to their dwellings, by driving sticks into the ground, which are so sharp at one end as to pierce the foot, and are generally dipt in poison. From what I can recollect of these battles, they appear to have been irruptions of one little state or district on the other, to obtain prisoners or booty. Perhaps they were incited to this by those traders who brought the European goods I mentioned amongst us. Such mode of obtaining slaves in Africa is common; and I believe more are procured this way, and by kidnapping, than any other. When a trader wants slaves, he applies to a chief for them, and tempts him with his wares. It is not extraordinary, if on this occasion he yields to the temptation with as little firmness, and accepts the price of his fellow creature's liberty with as little reluctance, as the enlightened merchant. Accordingly, he falls on his neighbours, and a desperate battle ensues. If he prevails, and takes prisoners, he gratifies his avarice by selling them; but, if his party be vanquished, and he falls into the hands of the enemy, he is put to death: for, as he has been known to foment their quarrels, it is thought dangerous to let him survive, and no ransom can save him, though all other prisoners may be redeemed. We have firearms, bows and arrows, broad two-edged swords and javelins; we have shields also, which cover a man from head to foot. All are taught the use of the weapons. Even our women are warriors, and march boldly out to fight along with the men. Our whole district is a kind of militia: on a certain signal given, such as the firing of a gun at night, they all rise in arms and rush upon their enemy. It is perhaps something remarkable, that when our people march to the field, a red flag or banner is borne before them. I was once a witness to a battle in our common. We had been all at work in it one day as usual when our people were suddenly attacked. I climbed a tree at some distance, from which I beheld the fight. There were many women as well as men on both sides; among others my mother was there and armed with a broad sword. After fighting for a considerable time with great fury, and many had been killed, our people obtained the victory, and took their enemy's Chief prisoner. He was carried off in great triumph, and, though he offered a large ransom for his life, he was put to death. A virgin of note among our enemies had been slain in the battle, and her arm was exposed in our market-place, where our trophies were always exhibited. The spoils were divided according to the merit of the warriors. Those prisoners which were not sold or redeemed we kept as slaves: but how different was their condition from that of the slaves in the West-Indies! With us they do no more work than other members of the community, even their master. Their food, cloathing, and lodging were nearly the same as theirs, except that they were not permitted to eat with those who were free born and there was scarce any other difference between them, than a superior degree of importance which the head of a family possesses in our state, and that authority which, as such, he exercises over every part of his household. Some of these slaves have even slaves under them, as their own property, and for their own use.

As to religion, the natives believe that there is one Creator of all things, and that he lives in the sun, and is girded round with a belt, that he may never eat or drink; but, according to some, he smokes a pipe, which is our own favourite luxury. They believe he governs events, especially our deaths or captivity; but, as for the doctrine of eternity, I do not remember to have ever heard of it: some however believe in the transmigration of souls in a certain degree. Those spirits, which are not transmigrated, such as our dear friends or relations, they believe always attend them, and guard them from the bad spirits of their foes. For this reason, they always, before eating, as I have observed, put some small portion of the meat, and pour some of their drink, on the ground for them; and they often make oblations of the blood of beasts or fowls at their graves. I was very fond of my mother, and almost constantly with her. When she went to make these oblations at her mother's tomb, which was a kind of small solitary thatched house, I sometimes attended her. There she made her libations, and spent most of the night in cries and lamentations. I have been often extremely terrified on these occasions. The loneliness of the place, the darkness of the night, and the ceremony of libation, naturally awful and gloomy, were heightened by my mother's lamentations; and these, concurring with the doleful cries of birds, by which these places were frequented, gave an inexpressible terror to the scene.

We compute the year from the day on which the sun crosses the line, and, on its setting that evening, there is a general shout throughout the land; at least I can speak from my own knowledge throughout our vicinity. The people at the same time make a great noise with rattles, not unlike the basket rattles used by children here, though much larger, and hold up their hands to heaven for a blessing. It is then the greatest offerings are made; and those children whom our wise men foretell will be fortunate are then presented to different people. I remember many used to come to see me, and I was carried about to others for that purpose. They have many offerings, particularly at full moons; generally two at harvest, before the fruits are taken out of the ground: and, when any young animals are killed, sometimes they offer up part of them as a sacrifice. These offerings, when made by one of the heads of a family, serve for the whole. I remember we often had them at my father's and my uncle's, and their families have been present. Some of our offerings are eaten with bitter herbs. We had a saying among us to any one of a cross temper, 'That if they were to be eaten, they should be eaten with bitter herbs.'

We practised circumcision like the Jews, and made offerings and feasts on that occasion in the same manner as they did. Like them also, our children were named from some event, some circumstance, or fancied foreboding at the time of their birth. I was named *Olaudah*, which, in our language, signifies vicissitude, or fortunate also; one favoured, and having a loud voice and well spoken. I remember we never polluted the name of the object of our adoration; on the contrary, it was always mentioned with the greatest reverence; and we were totally unacquainted with swearing, and all those terms of abuse and reproach which find the way so readily and copiously into the languages of more civilized people. The only expressions of that kind I remember were 'May you rot, or may you swell, or may a beast take you.'

I have before remarked, that the natives of this part of Africa are extremely cleanly. This necessary habit of decency was with us a part of religion, and therefore we had many purifications and washings; indeed almost as many, and used on the same occasions, if my recollection does not fail me, as the Jews. Those that touched the dead at any time were obliged to wash and purify themselves before they could enter a dwelling-house. Every woman too, at certain times, was forbidden to come into a dwelling-house, or touch any person, or any thing we ate. I was so fond of my mother I could not keep from her, or avoid touching her at some of those periods, in consequence of which I was obliged to be kept out with her, in a little house made for that purpose, till offering was made, and then we were purified.

Though we had no places of public worship, we had priests and magicians, or wise men. I do not remember whether they had different offices, or whether they were united in the same persons but they were held in great reverence by the people. They calculated our time, and foretold events, as their name imported, for we called them Ah-affoe-way-cah, which signifies calculators, or yearly men, our year being called Ah-affoe. They wore their beards; and, when they died, they were succeeded by their sons. Most of their implements and things of value were interred along with them. Pipes and tobacco were also put into the grave with the corpse, which was always perfumed and ornamented; and animals were offered in sacrifice to them. None accompanied their funerals but those of the same profession or tribe. These buried them after sunset, and always returned from the grave by a different way from that which they went.

These magicians were also our doctors or physicians. They practised bleeding by cupping, and were very successful in healing wounds and expelling poisons. They had likewise some extraordinary method of discovering jealousy, theft, and poisoning; the success of which no doubt they derived from their unbounded influence over the credulity and superstition of the people. I do not remember what those methods were, except that as to poisoning. I recollect an instance or two, which I hope it will not be deemed impertinent here to insert, as it may serve as a kind of specimen of the rest, and is still used by the negroes in the West Indies. A young woman had been poisoned, but it was not known by whom; the doctors ordered the corpse to be taken up by some persons, and carried to the grave. As soon as the bearers had raised it on their shoulders, they seemed seized with some sudden impulse, and ran to and fro', unable to stop themselves. At last, after having passed through a number of thorns and prickly bushes unhurt, the corpse fell from them close to a house, and defaced it in the fall: and the owner being taken up, he immediately confessed the poisoning.

The natives are extremely cautious about poison. When they buy any eatable the seller kisses it all round before the buyer, to shew him it is not poisoned; and the same is done when any meat or drink is presented, particularly to a stranger. We have serpents of different kinds, some of which are esteemed ominous when they appear in our houses, and these we never molest. I remember two of those ominous snakes, each of which was as thick as the calf of a man's leg, and in colour resembling a dolphin in the water, crept at different times into my mother's night-house, where I always lay with her, and coiled themselves into folds, and each time they crowed like a cock. I was desired by some of our wise men to touch these, that I might be interested in the good omens, which I did, for they were quite harmless, and would tamely suffer themselves to be handled; and then they were put into a large open earthen pan, and set on one side of the highway. Some of our snakes, however, were poisonous: one of them crossed the road one day when I was standing on it, and passed between my feet, without offering to touch me, to the great surprise of many who saw it; and these incidents were accounted by the wise men, and likewise by my mother and the rest of the people, as remarkable omens in my favour.

Such is the imperfect sketch my memory has furnished me with of the manners and customs of a people among whom I first drew my breath. And here I cannot forbear suggesting what has long struck me very forcibly, namely, the strong analogy which even by this sketch, imperfect as it is, appears to prevail in the manners and customs of my countrymen, and those of the Jews, before they reached the Land of Promise, and particularly the patriarchs, while they were yet in that pastoral state which is described in Genesis – an analogy, which alone would induce me to think that the one people had sprung from the other. Indeed this is the opinion of Dr Gill, who, in his commentary on Genesis, very ably deduces the pedigree of the Africans from Afer and Afra, the descendants of Abraham by Keturah his wife and concubine, (for both these titles are applied to her). It is also conformable to the sentiments of Dr John Clarke, formerly Dean of Sarum, in his Truth of the Christian Religion: both these authors concur in ascribing to us this original. The reasonings of these gentlemen are still further confirmed by the

Scripture Chronology of the Rev. Arthur Bedford; and if any further corroboration were required, this resemblance in so many respects is a strong evidence in support of the opinion. Like the Israelites in their primitive state, our government was conducted by our chiefs, our judges, our wise men, and elders; and the head of a family with us enjoyed a similar authority over his household with that which is ascribed to Abraham and the other patriarchs. The law of retaliation obtained almost universally with us as with them: and even their religion appeared to have shed upon us a ray of its glory, though broken and spent in its passage, or eclipsed by the cloud with which time, tradition, and ignorance might have enveloped it: for we had our circumcision (a rule I believe peculiar to that people): we had also our sacrifices and burnt-offerings, our washings and purifications, on the same occasions as they had.

As to the difference of colour between the Eboan Africans and the modern Jews, I shall not presume to account for it. It is a subject which has engaged the pens of men of both genius and learning, and is far above my strength. The most able and Reverend Mr T. Clarkson, however, in his much-admired Essay on the Slavery and Commerce of the Human Species, has ascertained the cause, in a manner that at once solves every objection on that account, and, on my mind at least, has produced the fullest conviction. I shall therefore refer to that performance for the theory, contenting myself with extracting a fact as related by Dr Mitchel. 'The Spaniards, who have inhabited America, under the torrid zone, for any time, are become as dark coloured as our native Indians of Virginia, *of which I myself have been a witness*. There is also another instance of a Portuguese settlement at Mitomba, a river in Sierra Leona, where the inhabitants are bred from a mixture of the first Portuguese discoverers with the natives, and are now become, in their complexion, and in the woolly quality of their hair, *perfect negroes*, retaining however a smattering of the Portuguese language.'

These instances, and a great many more which might be adduced, while they shew how the complexions of the same persons vary in different climates, it is hoped may tend also to remove the prejudice that some conceive against the natives of Africa on account of their colour. Surely the minds of the Spaniards did not change with their complexions! Are there not causes enough to which the apparent inferiority of an African may be ascribed, without limiting the goodness of God, and supposing he forbore to stamp understanding on certainly his own image, because 'carved in ebony?' Might it not naturally be ascribed to their situation? When they come among Europeans, they are ignorant of their language, religion, manners, and customs. Are any pains taken to teach them these? Are they treated as men? Does not slavery itself depress the mind, and extinguish all its fire, and every noble sentiment? But, above all, what advantages do not a refined people possess over those who are rude and uncultivated? Let the polished and haughty European recollect that *his* ancestors were once, like the Africans, uncivilized, and even barbarous. Did Nature make *them* inferior to their sons? and should *they too* have been made slaves? Every rational mind answers, No. Let such reflections as these melt the pride of their superiority into sympathy for the wants and miseries of their sable brethren, and compel them to acknowledge, that understanding is not confined to feature or colour. If, when they look round the world, they feel exultation, let it be tempered with benevolence to others, and gratitude to God, 'who hath made of one blood all nations of men for to dwell on all the face of the earth; and whose wisdom is not our wisdom, neither are our ways his ways.'

2. Kidnap

I hope the reader will not think I have trespassed on his patience in introducing myself to him with some account of the manners and customs of my country. They had been implanted in me with great care, and made an impression on my mind, which time could not erase, and which all the adversity and variety of fortune I have since experienced served only to rivet and record: for, whether the love of one's country be real or imaginary, or a lesson of reason, or an instinct of nature, I still look back with pleasure on the first scenes of my life, though that pleasure has been for the most part mingled with sorrow.

I have already acquainted the reader with the time and place of my birth. My father, besides many slaves, had a numerous family, of which seven lived to grow up, including myself and a sister, who was the only daughter. As I was the youngest of the sons, I became, of course, the greatest favourite with my mother, and was always with her; and she used to take particular pains to form my mind. I was trained up from my earliest years in the arts of agriculture and war: my daily exercise was shooting and throwing javelins; and my mother adorned me with emblems, after the manner of our greatest warriors. In this way I grew up till I was turned the age of eleven, when an end was put to my happiness in the following manner: – Generally, when the grown people in the neighbourhood were gone far in the fields to labour, the children assembled together in some of the neighbours' premises to play; and commonly some of us used to get up a tree to look out for any assailant, or kidnapper, that might come upon us; for they sometimes took those opportunities of our parents' absence, to attack and carry off as many as they could seize. One day, as I was watching at the top of a tree in our yard, I saw one of those people come into the yard of our next neighbour but one, to kidnap, there being many stout young people in it. Immediately, on this, I gave the alarm of the rogue, and he was surrounded by the stoutest of them, who entangled him with cords, so that he could not escape till some of the grown people came and secured him. But, alas! ere long it was my fate to be thus attacked, and to be carried off, when none of the grown people were nigh. One day, when all our people were gone out to their works as usual, and only I and my dear sister were left to mind the house, two men and a woman got over our walls, and in a moment seized us both; and, without giving us time to cry out, or make resistance, they stopped our mouths, tied our hands, and ran off with us into the nearest wood: and con-tinued to carry us as far as they could, till night came on, when we reached a small house, where the robbers halted for refreshment, and spent the night. We were then unbound, but were unable to take any food; and, being quite overpowered by fatigue and grief, our only relief was some sleep, which allayed our misfortune for a short time. The next morning we left the house, and continued travelling all the day. For a long time we had kept to the woods, but at last we came into a road which I believed I knew. I had now some hopes of being delivered; for we had advanced but a little way before I discovered some people at a distance, on which I began to cry out for their assistance; but my cries had no other effect than to make them tie me faster, and stop my mouth, and then they put me into a large sack. They also stopped my sister's mouth, and tied her hands; and in this manner we proceeded till we were out of the sight of these people. – When we went to rest the following night they offered us some victuals; but we refused them; and the only comfort we had was in being in one another's arms all that night, and bathing each other with our tears. But, alas! we were soon deprived of even the smallest comfort of weeping together. The next day proved a day of greater sorrow than I had yet experienced; for my sister and I were then separated, while we lay clasped in each other's arms. It was in vain that we besought them not to part us: she was torn from me, and immediately carried away, while I was left in a state of distraction not to be described. I cried and grieved continually; and for several days I did not eat any thing but what they forced into my mouth. At length, after many days' travelling, during which I had often changed masters, I got into the hands of a chieftain, in a very pleasant country. This man had two wives and some children, and they all used me extremely well, and did all they could to comfort me; particularly the first wife, who

23

was something like my mother. Although I was a great many days' journey from my father's house, yet these people spoke exactly the same language with us. This first master of mine, as I may call him, was a smith, and my principal employment was working his bellows, which were the same kind as I had seen in my vicinity. They were in some respects not unlike the stoves here in gentlemen's kitchens; and were covered over with leather; and in the middle of that leather a stick was fixed, and a person stood up, and worked it, in the same manner as is done to pump water out of a cask with a hand-pump. I believe it was gold he worked, for it was of a lovely bright yellow colour, and was worn by the women on their wrists and ancles. I was there I suppose about a month, and they at last used to trust me some little distance from the house. This liberty I used in embracing every opportunity to inquire the way to my own home: and I also sometimes, for the same purpose, went with the maidens, in the cool of the evenings, to bring pitchers of water from the springs for the use of the house. I had also remarked where the sun rose in the morning, and set in the evening, as I had travelled along; and I had observed that my father's house was towards the rising of the sun. I therefore determined to seize the first opportunity of making my escape, and to shape my course for that quarter; for I was quite oppressed and weighed down by grief after my mother and friends; and my love of liberty, ever great, was strengthened by the mortifying circumstance of not daring to eat with the free-born children, although I was mostly their companion.

– While I was projecting my escape one day, an unlucky event happened, which quite disconcerted my plan, and put an end to my hopes. I used to be sometimes employed in assisting an elderly woman slave to cook and take care of the poultry; and one morning, while I was feeding some chickens, I happened to toss a small pebble at one of them, which hit it on the middle, and directly killed it. The old slave, having soon after missed the chicken, inquired after it; and on my relating the accident (for I told her the truth, because my mother would never suffer me to tell a lie) she flew into a violent passion, threatened that I should suffer for it; and, my master being out, she immediately went and told her mistress what I had done. This alarmed me very much, and I expected an instant correction, which to me was uncommonly dreadful; for I had seldom been beaten at home. I therefore resolved to fly; and accordingly I ran into a thicket that was hard by, and hid myself in the bushes. Soon afterwards my mistress and the slave returned, and, not seeing me, they searched all the house, but, not finding me, and I not making answer when they called to me, they thought I had run away, and the whole neighbourhood was raised in the pursuit of me. In that part of the country (as well as ours) the houses and villages were skirted with woods, or shrubberies, and the bushes were so thick, that a man could readily conceal himself in them, so as to elude the strictest search. The neighbours continued the whole day looking for me, and several times many of them came within a few yards of the place where I lay hid. I expected every moment when I heard a rustling among the trees, to be found out, and punished by my master; but they never discovered me, though they were often so near that I even heard their conjectures as they were looking about for me; and I now learned from them, that any attempt to return home would be hopeless. Most of them supposed I had fled towards home; but the distance was so great, and the way so intricate, that they thought I could never reach it, and that I should be lost in the woods. When I heard this I was seized with a violent panic, and abandoned myself to despair. Night too began to approach, and aggravated all my fears. I had before entertained hopes of getting home, and I had determined when it should be dark to make the attempt; but I was now convinced it was fruitless, and I began to consider that, if possibly I could escape all other animals, I could not those of the human kind; and that, not knowing the way, I must perish in the woods.

I heard frequent rustlings among the leaves; and, being pretty sure they were snakes, I expected every instant to be stung by them. – This increased my anguish, and the horror of my situation became now quite insupportable. I at length quitted the thicket, very faint and hungry, for I had not eaten or drank any thing all the day, and crept to my master's kitchen, from whence I set out at first, and which was an open shed, and laid myself down in the ashes, with an anxious wish for death to relieve me from all my pains. I was scarcely awake in the morning when the old woman slave, who was the first up, came to light the fire, and saw me in the fire-place. She was very much surprised to see me, and could scarcely believe her own eyes. She now promised to intercede for me, and went for her master, who soon after came, and, having slightly reprimanded me, ordered me to be taken care of, and not ill-treated.

Soon after this my master's only daughter and child by his first wife sickened and died, which affected him so much that for some time he was almost frantic, and really would have killed himself had he not been watched and prevented. However, in a small time afterwards he recovered, and I was again sold. I was now carried to the left of the sun's rising, through many dreary wastes and dismal woods, amidst the hideous roarings of wild beasts. – The people I was sold to used to carry me very often, when I was tired, either on their shoulders or on their backs. I saw many convenient well-built sheds along the roads, at proper distances, to accommodate the merchants and travellers, who lay in those buildings along with their wives, who often accompany them; and they always go well armed.

From the time I left my own nation I always found somebody that understood me till I came to the sea coast. The languages of different nations did not totally differ, nor were they so copious as those of the Europeans, particularly the English. They were therefore easily learned; and, while I was journeying thus through Africa, I acquired two or three different tongues. In this manner I had been travelling for a considerable time, when one evening, to my great surprise, whom should I see brought to the house where I was but my dear sister. As soon as she saw me she gave a loud shriek, and ran into my arms. – I was quite overpowered; neither of us could speak, but, for a considerable time, clung to each other in mutual embraces, unable to do any thing but weep. Our meeting affected all who saw us; and indeed I must acknowledge, in honour of those sable destroyers of human rights, that I never met with any ill treatment, or saw any offered to their slaves, except tying them, when necessary, to keep them from running away. When these people knew we were brother and sister they indulged us to be together; and the man, to whom I supposed we belonged, lay with us, he in the middle, while she and I held one another by the hands across his breast all night; and thus for a while we forgot our misfortunes in the joy of being together: but even this small comfort was soon to have an end; for scarcely had the fatal morning appeared, when she was again torn from me for ever! I was now more miserable, if possible, than before. The small relief which her presence gave me from pain was gone, and the wretchedness of my situation was redoubled by my anxiety after her fate, and my apprehensions lest her sufferings should be greater than mine, when I could not be with her to alleviate them. Yes, thou dear partner of all my childish sports! thou sharer of my joys and sorrows! happy should I have ever esteemed myself to encounter every misery for you, and to procure your freedom by the sacrifice of my own. Though you were early forced from my arms, your image has been always rivetted in my heart, from which neither *time nor fortune* have been able to remove it: so that, while the thoughts of your sufferings have damped my prosperity, they have mingled with adversity, and increased its bitterness. – To that heaven which protects the weak from the strong, I commit the care of your innocence and virtues, if they have not already received their full reward; and if your youth and delicacy have not long since fallen victims to the violence of the African trader, the pestilential stench of a Guinea ship, the seasoning in the European colonies, or the lash and lust of a brutal and unrelenting overseer.

I did not long remain after my sister. I was again sold, and carried through a number of places, till, after travelling a considerable time, I came to a town called Tinmah, in the most beautiful country I had yet seen in Africa. It was extremely rich, and there were many rivulets which flowed through it; and supplied a large pond in the center of the town, where the people washed. Here I first saw and tasted cocoa nuts, which I thought superior to any nuts I had ever tasted before; and the trees, which were loaded, were also interspersed amongst the houses, which had commodious shades adjoining, and were in the same manner as ours, the insides being neatly plastered and whitewashed. Here I also saw and tasted for the first time sugar-cane. Their money consisted of little white shells, the size of the finger nail: they are known in this country by the name of *core*. I was sold here for one hundred and seventy-two of them by a merchant who lived and brought me there. I had been about two or three days at his house, when a wealthy widow, a neighbour of his, came there one evening, and brought with her an only son, a young gentleman about my own age and size. Here they saw me; and, having taken a fancy to me, I was bought of the merchant, and went home with them. Her house and premises were situated close to one of those rivulets I have mentioned, and were the finest I ever saw in Africa: they were very extensive, and she had a number of slaves to attend her. The next day I was washed and perfumed, and when meal-time came, I was led into the presence of my mistress, and ate and drank before her with her son. This filled me with astonishment: and I could scarce help expressing my surprise that the young gentleman should suffer me, who was bound, to eat with him who was free; and not only so, but that he would not at any time either eat or drink till I had taken first, because I was the eldest, which was agreeable to our custom. Indeed every thing here, and all their treatment of me, made me forget that I was a slave. The language of these people resembled ours so nearly, that we understood each other perfectly. They had also the very same customs as we. There were likewise slaves daily to attend us, while my young master and I, with other boys, sported with our darts and bows and arrows, as I had been used to do at home. In this resemblance to my former happy state I passed about two months, and I now began to think I was to be adopted into the family, and was beginning to be reconciled to my situation, and to forget by degrees my misfortunes, when all at once the delusion vanished; for, without the least previous knowledge, one morning early, while my dear master and companion was still asleep, I was awakened out of my reverie to fresh sorrow, and hurried away even among the uncircumcised.

Thus, at the very moment I dreamed of the greatest happiness, I found myself most miserable: and it seemed as if fortune wished to give me this taste of joy only to render the reverse more poignant. The change I now experienced was as painful as it was sudden and unexpected. It was a change indeed from a state of bliss to a scene which is inexpressible by me, as it discovered to me an element I had never before beheld, and till then had no idea of, and wherein such instances of hardship and cruelty continually occurred as I can never reflect on but with horror.

All the nations and people I had hitherto passed through resembled our own in their manners, customs and language: but I came at length to a country, the inhabitants of which differed from us in all those particulars. I was very much struck with this difference, especially when I came among a people who did not circumcise, and eat without washing their hands. They cooked also in iron pots, and had European cutlasses and cross bows, which were unknown to us, and fought with their fists among themselves. Their women were not so modest as ours, for they eat, and drank, and slept with their men. But, above all, I was amazed to see no sacrifices or offerings among them. In some of those places the people ornamented themselves with scars, and likewise filed their teeth very sharp. They wanted sometimes to ornament me in the same manner, but I would not suffer them; hoping that I might some time be among a people who did not thus disfigure themselves, as I thought they did. At last, I came to the banks of a large river, which was covered with canoes, in which the people appeared to live with their household utensils and provisions of all kinds. I was beyond measure astonished at this, as I had never before seen any water larger than a pond or a rivulet; and my surprise was mingled with no small fear when I was put into one of these canoes, and we began to paddle and move along the river. We continued going on thus till night; and when we came to land, and made fires on the banks, each family by themselves, some dragged their canoes on shore, others staid and cooked in theirs, and laid in them all night. Those on the land had mats, of which they made tents, some in the shape of little houses: In these we slept; and after the morning meal we embarked again, and proceeded as before. I was often very much astonished to see some of the women, as well as the men, jump into the water, dive to the bottom, come up again, and swim about. Thus I continued to travel, sometimes by land, sometimes by water, through different countries, and various nations, till, at the end of six or seven months after I had been kidnapped, I arrived at the sea coast. It would be tedious and uninteresting to relate all the incidents which befel me during this journey, and which I have not yet forgotten; of the various hands I passed through, and the manners and customs of all the different people among whom I lived: I shall therefore only observe, that, in all the places where I was, the soil was exceedingly rich; the pomkins, eadas, plantains, yams, &c. &c. were in great abundance, and of incredible size. There were also vast quantities of different gums, though not used for any purpose; and every where a great deal of tobacco. The cotton even grew quite wild; and there was plenty of red wood. I saw no mechanics whatever in all the way, except such as I have mentioned. The chief employment in all these countries was agriculture, and both the males and females, as with us, were brought up to it, and trained in the arts of war.

The first object which saluted my eyes when I arrived on the coast was the sea, and a slave-ship, which was then riding at anchor, and waiting for its cargo. These filled me with astonishment, which was soon converted into terror, which I am yet at a loss to describe, nor the then feelings of my mind. When I was carried on board I was immediately handled, and tossed up, to see if I were sound, by some of the crew; and I was now persuaded that I had gotten into a world of bad spirits, and that they were going to kill me. Their complexions too differing so much from ours, their long hair, and the language they spoke, which was very different from any I had ever heard, united to confirm me in this belief. Indeed, such were the horrors of my views and fears at the moment, that, if ten thousand worlds had been my own, I would have freely parted with them all to have exchanged my condition with that of the meanest slave in my own country. When I looked round the ship too, and saw a large furnace of copper boiling, and a multitude of black people of every description chained together, every one of their countenances expressing dejection and sorrow, I no longer doubted of my fate, and, quite overpowered with horror and anguish, I fell motionless on the deck and fainted. When I recovered a little, I found some black people about me, who I believed were some of those who brought me on board, and had been receiving their pay; they talked to me in order to cheer me, but all in vain. I asked them if we were not to be eaten by those white men with horrible looks, red faces, and long hair? They told me I was not; and one of the crew brought me a small portion of spirituous liquor in a wine glass; but, being afraid of him, I would not take it out of his hand. One of the blacks therefore took it from him and gave it to me, and I took a little down my palate, which, instead of reviving me, as they thought it would, threw me into the greatest consternation at the strange feeling it produced, having never tasted any such liquor before. Soon after this, the blacks who brought me on board went off, and left me abandoned to despair. I now saw myself deprived of all chance of returning to my native country, or even the least glimpse of hope of gaining the shore, which I now considered as friendly: and I even wished for my former slavery in preference to my present situation, which was filled with horrors of every kind, still heightened by my ignorance of what I was to undergo. I was not long suffered to indulge my grief; I was soon put down under the decks, and there I received such a salutation in my nostrils as I had never experienced in my life; so that with the loathsomeness of the stench, and crying together, I became so sick and low that I was not able to eat, nor had I the least desire to taste any thing. I now wished for the last friend, Death, to relieve me; but soon, to my grief, two of the white men offered me eatables; and, on my refusing to eat, one of them held me fast by the hands, and laid me across, I think, the windlass, and tied my feet, while the other flogged me severely. I had never experienced any thing of this kind before; and although, not being used to the water, I naturally feared that element the first time I saw it; yet, nevertheless, could I have got over the nettings, I would have jumped over the side, but I could not; and, besides, the crew used to watch us very closely who were not chained down to the decks, lest we should leap into the water; and I have seen some of these poor African prisoners most severely cut for attempting to do so, and hourly whipped for not eating. This indeed was often the case with myself. In a little time after, amongst the poor chained men, I found some of my own nation, which in a small degree gave ease to my mind. I inquired of these what was to be done with us? they gave me to understand we were to be carried to these white people's country to work for them. I then was a little revived, and thought, if it were no worse than working, my situation was not so desperate: but still I feared I should be put to death, the white people looked and acted, as I thought, in so savage a manner; for I had never seen among any people such instances of brutal cruelty; and this not only shewn towards us blacks, but also to some of the whites themselves. One white man in particular I saw, when we were permitted to be on deck, flogged so unmercifully with a large rope near the foremast, that he died in consequence of it; and they tossed him over the side as they would have done a brute. This made me fear these people the more; and I expected nothing less than to be treated in the same manner. I could not help expressing my fears and apprehensions to some of my countrymen: I asked them if these people had no country, but lived in this hollow place the ship? they told me they did not, but came from a distant one. 'Then,' said I, 'how comes it in all our country we never heard of them?' They told me, because they lived so very far off. I then asked where were their women? had they any like themselves? I was told they had: 'And why,' said I, 'do we not see them?' they answered, because they were left behind. I asked how the vessel could go? they told me they could not tell; but that there were cloths put upon the masts by the help of the ropes I saw, and then the vessel went on; and the white men had some spell or magic they put in the water when they liked in order to stop the vessel. I was exceedingly amazed at this account, and really thought they were spirits. I therefore wished much to be from amongst them, for I expected they would sacrifice me: but my wishes were vain; for we were so quartered that it was impossible for any of us to make our escape. While we staid on the coast I was mostly on deck; and one day, to my great astonishment, I saw one of these vessels coming in with the sails up. As soon as the whites saw it, they gave a great shout, at which we were amazed; and the more so as the vessel appeared larger by approaching nearer. At last she came to an anchor in my sight, and when the anchor was let go, I and my countrymen who saw it were lost in astonishment to observe the vessel stop; and were now convinced it was done by magic. Soon after this the other ship got her boats out, and they came on board of us, and the people of both ships seemed very glad to see each other. Several of the strangers also shook hands with us black people, and made motions with their hands, signifying, I suppose, we were to go to their country; but we did not understand them. At last, when the ship we were in had got in all her cargo, they made ready with many fearful noises, and we were all put under deck, so that we could not see how they managed the vessel. But this disappointment was the least of my sorrow. The stench of the hold while we were on the coast was so intolerably loathsome, that it was dangerous to remain there for any time, and some of us had been permitted to stay on the deck for the fresh air; but now that the whole ship's cargo were confined together, it became absolutely pestilential. The closeness of the place, and the heat of the climate, added to the number in the ship, which was so crowded that each had scarcely room to turn himself, almost suffocated us. This produced copious perspirations, so that the air soon became unfit for respiration, from a variety of loathsome smells, and brought on a sickness among the slaves, of which many died, thus falling victims to the improvident avarice, as I may call it, of their purchasers. This wretched situation was again aggravated by the galling of the chains, now become insupportable; and the filth of the necessary tubs, into which the children often fell, and were almost suffocated. The shrieks of the women, and the groans of the dying, rendered the whole a scene of horror almost inconceiveable. Happily perhaps for myself I was soon reduced so low here that it was thought necessary to keep me almost always on deck; and from my extreme youth I was not put in fetters. In this situation I expected every hour to share the fate of my companions, some of whom were almost daily brought upon deck at the point of death, which I began to hope would soon put an end to my miseries. Often did I think many of the inhabitants of the deep much more happy than myself; I envied them the freedom they enjoyed, and as often wished I could change my condition for theirs. Every circumstance I met with served only to render my state more painful, and heighten my apprehensions, and my opinion of the cruelty of the whites. One day they had taken a number of fishes; and when they had killed and satisfied themselves with as many as they thought fit, to our astonishment who were on the deck, rather than give any of them to us to eat, as we expected, they tossed the remaining fish into the sea again, although we begged and prayed for some as well as we could, but in vain; and some of my countrymen, being pressed by hunger, took an opportunity, when they thought no one saw them, of trying to get a little privately; but they were discovered, and the attempt procured them some very severe floggings.

One day, when we had a smooth sea, and moderate wind, two of my wearied countrymen, who were chained together (I was near them at the time), preferring death to such a life of misery, somehow made through the nettings, and jumped into the sea: immediately another quite dejected fellow, who, on account of his illness, was suffered to be out of irons, also followed their example; and I believe many more would very soon have done the same, if they had not been prevented by the ship's crew, who were instantly alarmed. Those of us that were the most active were, in a moment, put down under the deck; and there was such a noise and confusion amongst the people of the ship as I never heard before, to stop her, and get the boat out to go after the slaves. However, two of the wretches were drowned, but they got the other, and afterwards flogged him unmercifully, for thus attempting to prefer death to slavery. In this manner we continued to undergo more hardships than I can now relate; hardships which are inseparable from this accursed trade. – Many a time we were near suffocation, from the want of fresh air, which we were often without for whole days together. This, and the stench of the necessary tubs, carried off many. During our passage I first saw flying fishes, which surprised me very much: they used frequently to fly across the ship, and many of them fell on the deck. I also now first saw the use of the quadrant. I had often with astonishment seen the mariners make observations with it, and I could not think what it meant. They at last took notice of my surprise; and one of them, willing to increase it, as well as to gratify my curiosity, made me one day look through it. The clouds appeared to me to be land, which disappeared as they passed along. This heightened my wonder: and I was now more persuaded than ever that I was in another world, and that every thing about me was magic. At last we came in sight of the island of Barbadoes, at which the whites on board gave a great shout, and made many signs of joy to us. We did not know what to think of this; but as the vessel drew nearer we plainly saw the harbour, and other ships of different kinds and sizes: and we soon anchored amongst them off Bridge Town. Many merchants and planters now came on board, though it was in the evening. They put us in separate parcels, and examined us attentively. They also made us jump, and pointed to the land, signifying we were to go there. We thought by this we should be eaten by these ugly men, as they appeared to us; and, when soon after we were all put down under the deck again, there was much dread and trembling among us, and nothing but bitter cries to be heard all the night from these apprehensions, insomuch that at last the white people got some old slaves from the land to pacify us. They told us we were not to be eaten, but to work, and were soon to go on land, where we should see many of our country people. This report eased us much; and sure enough, soon after we were landed, there came to us Africans of all languages. We were conducted immediately to the merchant's yard, where we were all pent up together like so many sheep in a fold, without regard to sex or age. As every object was new to me, every thing I saw filled me with surprise. What struck me first was, that the houses were built with bricks, in storeys, and in every other respect different from those in I have seen in Africa: but I was still more astonished on seeing people on horseback. I did not know what this could mean; and indeed I thought these people were full of nothing but magical arts. While I was in this astonishment, one of my fellow prisoners spoke to a countryman of his about the horses, who said they were the same kind they had in their country. I understood them, though they were from a distant part of Africa, and I thought it odd I had not seen any horses there; but afterwards, when I came to converse with different Africans, I found they had many horses amongst them, and much larger than those I then saw. We were not many days in the merchant's custody before we were sold after their usual manner, which is this: – On a signal given, (as the beat of a drum), the buyers rush at once into the yard where the slaves are confined, and make choice of that parcel they like best. The noise and clamour with which this is attended, and the eagerness visible in the countenances of the buyers, serve not a little to increase the apprehensions of the terrified Africans, who may well be supposed to consider them as the ministers of that destruction to which they think themselves devoted. In this manner, without scruple, are relations and friends separated, most of them never to see each other again. I remember in the vessel in which I was brought over, in the men's apartment, there were several brothers, who, in the sale, were sold in different lots; and it was very moving on this occasion to see and hear their cries at parting. O, ye nominal Christians! might not an African ask you, learned you this from your God? Who says unto you, Do unto all men as you would men should do unto you? Is it not enough that we are torn from our country and friends to toil for your luxury and lust of gain? Must every tender feeling be likewise sacrificed to your avarice? Are the dearest friends and relations, now rendered more dear by their separation from their kindred, still to be parted from each other, and thus prevented from cheering the gloom of slavery with the small comfort of being together and mingling their sufferings and sorrows? Why are parents to lose their children, brothers their sisters, or husbands their wives? Surely this is a new refinement in cruelty, which, while it has no advantage to atone for it, thus aggravates distress, and adds fresh horrors even to the wretchedness of slavery.

3. *The Iron Muzzle*

I now totally lost the small remains of comfort I had enjoyed in conversing with my countrymen; the women too, who used to wash and take care of me, were all gone different ways, and I never saw one of them afterwards.

I stayed in this island for a few days; I believe it could not be above a fortnight; when I and some few more slaves, that were not saleable among the rest, from very much fretting, were shipped off in a sloop for North America. On the passage we were better treated than when we were coming from Africa, and we had plenty of rice and fat pork. We were landed up a river a good way from the sea, about Virginia county, where we saw few or none of our native Africans, and not one soul who could talk to me. I was a few weeks weeding grass, and gathering stones in a plantation; and at last all my companions were distributed different ways, and only myself was left. I was now exceedingly miserable, and thought myself worse off than any of the rest of my companions; for they could talk to each other, but I had no person to speak to that I could understand. In this state I was constantly grieving and pining, and wishing for death, rather than any thing else. While I was in this plantation, the gentleman, to whom I supposed the estate belonged, being unwell, I was one day sent for to his dwelling house to fan him: when I came into the room where he was, I was very much affrighted at some things I saw, and the more so as I had seen a black woman slave as I came through the house, who was cooking the dinner, and the poor creature was cruelly loaded with various kinds of iron machines; she had one particularly on her head, which locked her mouth so fast that she could scarcely speak; and could not eat nor drink. I was much astonished and shocked at this contrivance, which I afterwards learned was called the iron muzzle. Soon after I had a fan put into my hand, to fan the gentleman while he slept; and so I did indeed with great fear. While he was fast asleep I indulged myself a great deal in looking about the room, which to me appeared very fine and curious. The first object that engaged my attention was a watch which hung on the chimney, and was going. I was quite surprised at the noise it made, and was afraid it would tell the gentleman any thing I might do amiss: and when I immediately after observed a picture hanging in the room, which appeared constantly to look at me, I was still more affrighted, having never seen such things as these before. At one time I thought it was something relative to magic; and not seeing it move, I thought it might be some way the whites had to keep their great men when they died, and offer them libations as we used to do our friendly spirits. In this state of anxiety I remained till my master awoke, when I was dismissed out of the room, to my no small satisfaction and relief, for I thought that these people were all made of wonders. In this place I was called Jacob; but on board the African snow I was called Michael. I had been some time in this miserable, forlorn, and much dejected state, without having any one to talk to, which made my life a burden, when the kind and unknown hand of the Creator (who in very deed leads the blind in a way they know not) now began to appear, to my comfort; for one day the captain of a merchant ship, called the Industrious Bee, came on some business to my master's house. This gentleman, whose name was Michael Henry Pascal, was a lieutenant in the royal navy, but now commanded this trading ship, which was somewhere in the confines of the county many miles off. While he was at my master's house it happened that he saw me, and liked me so well that he made a purchase of me. I think I have often heard him say he gave thirty or forty pounds sterling for me; but I do not now remember which. However, he meant me for a present to some of his friends in England; and I was sent accordingly from the house of my then master (one Mr Campbell) to the place where the ship lay; I was conducted on horseback by an elderly black man (a mode of travelling which appeared very odd to me). When I arrived I was carried on board a fine large ship, loaded with tobacco, &c. and just ready to sail for England. I now thought my condition much mended; I had sails to lie on, and plenty of good victuals to eat; and every body on board used me very kindly, quite contrary to what I had seen of any white people before; I therefore began to think that they were not all of the same disposition. A few days after I was on board we sailed for England. I was still at a loss to conjecture my destiny. By this time, however, I could smatter a little imperfect English; and I wanted to know as well as I could where we were going. Some of the people of the ship used to tell me they were going to carry me back to my own country; and this made me very happy. I was quite rejoiced at the idea of going back; and thought if I should get home what wonders I should have to tell. But I was reserved for another fate and was soon undeceived when we came within sight of the English coast. While I was on board this ship, my captain and master named me *Gustavus Vasa*. I at that time began to understand him a little, and refused to be called so, and told him as well as I could that I would be called Jacob; but he said I should not, and still called me Gustavus; and when I refused to answer to my new name, which at first I did, it gained me many a cuff; so at length I submitted, and by which I have been known ever since. The ship had a very long passage; and on that account we had very short allowance of provisions. Towards the last we had only one pound and a half of bread per week, and about the same quantity of meat, and one quart of water a day. We spoke with only one vessel the whole time we were at sea, and but once we caught a few fishes. In our extremities the captain and people told me in jest they would kill and eat me, but I thought them in earnest, and was depressed beyond measure, expecting every moment to be my last. While I was in this situation one evening they caught, with a good deal of trouble, a large shark, and got it on board. This gladdened my poor heart exceedingly, as I thought it would serve the people to eat instead of their eating me; but very soon, to my astonishment, they cut off a small part of the tail, and tossed the rest over the side. This renewed my consternation; and I did not know what to think of these white people; I very much feared they would kill and eat me. There was on board the ship a young lad who had never been at sea before, about four or five years older than myself: his name was Richard Baker. He was a native of America, had received an excellent education, and was of a most amiable temper. Soon after I went on board he shewed me a great deal of partiality and attention, and in return I grew extremely fond of him. We at length became inseparable; and for the space of two years, he was of very great use to me, and was my constant companion and instructor. Although this dear youth had many slaves of his own, yet he and I have gone through many sufferings together on shipboard; and we have many nights lain in each other's bosoms when we were in great distress. Thus such a friendship was cemented between us as we cherished till his death, which, to my very great sorrow, happened in the year 1759, when he was up the Archipelago, on board His Majesty's ship the *Preston*: an event which I have never ceased to regret, as I lost at once a kind interpreter, an agreeable companion, and a faithful friend; who, at the age of fifteen, discovered a mind superior to prejudice; and who was not ashamed to notice, to associate with, and to be the friend and instructor of one who was ignorant, a stranger, of a different complexion, and a slave! My master had lodged in his mother's house in America: he respected him very much, and made him always eat with him in the cabin. He used often to tell him jocularly that he would kill and eat me. Sometimes he would say to me – the black people were not good to eat, and would ask me if we did not eat people in my country. I said, No: then he said he would kill Dick (as he always called him) first, and afterwards me. Though this hearing relieved my mind a little as to myself, I was alarmed for Dick, and whenever he was called I used to be very much afraid he was to be killed; and I would peep and watch to see if they were going to kill him: nor was I free from this consternation till we made the land. One night we lost a man overboard; and the cries and noise were so great and confused, in stopping the ship, that I, who did not know what was the matter, began, as usual, to be very much afraid, and to think they were going to make an offering with me, and perform some magic; which I still believed they dealt in. As the waves were very high, I thought the Ruler of the seas was angry, and I expected to be offered up to appease him. This filled my mind with agony, and I could not any more that night close my eyes again to rest. However, when day-light appeared, I was a little eased in my mind; but still every time I was called I used to think it was to be killed. Some time after this we saw some very large fish, which I afterwards found were called grampusses. They looked to me extremely terrible, and made their appearance just at dusk, and were so near as to blow the water on the ship's deck. I believed them to be the rulers of the sea; and, as the white people did not make any offerings at any time, I thought they were angry with them; and, at last, what confirmed my belief was, the wind just then died away, and a calm ensued, and in consequence of it the ship stopped going. I supposed that the fish had performed this, and I hid myself in the fore-part of the ship, through fear of being offered up to appease them, every minute peeping and quaking; but my good friend Dick came shortly towards me, and I took an opportunity to ask him, as well as I could, what these fish were? not being able to talk much English, I could but just make him understand my question; and not at all, when I asked him if any offerings were to be made to them? However, he told me these fish would swallow any body; which sufficiently alarmed me. Here he was called away by the captain, who was leaning over the quarter-deck railing and looking at the fish; and most of the people were busied in getting a barrel of pitch to light, for them to play with. The captain now called me to him, having learned some of my apprehensions from Dick; and having diverted himself and others for some time with my fears, which appeared ludicrous enough in my crying and trembling, he dismissed me. The barrel of pitch was now lighted and put over the side into the water: by this time it was just dark, and the fish went after it; and, to my great joy, I saw them no more.

However, all my alarms began to subside when we got sight of land; and at last the ship arrived at Falmouth, after a passage of thirteen weeks. Every heart on board seemed gladdened on our reaching the shore, and none more than mine. The captain immediately went on shore, and sent on board some fresh provisions, which we wanted very much: we made good use of them, and our famine was soon turned into feasting, almost without ending. It was about the beginning of the spring 1757 when I arrived in England, and I was near twelve years of age at that time. I was very much struck with the buildings and the pavement of the streets in Falmouth; and, indeed, any object I saw filled me with new surprise. One morning, when I got upon deck, I saw it covered all over with the snow that fell over-night: as I had never seen any thing of the kind before, I thought it was salt; so I immediately ran down to the mate, and desired him, as well as I could, to come and see how somebody in the night had thrown salt all over the deck. He, knowing what it was, desired me to bring some of it down to him: accordingly I took up a handful of it, which I found very cold indeed; and when I brought it to him he desired me to taste it. I did so, and I was surprised beyond measure. I then asked him what it was? he told me it was snow: but I could not in any wise understand him. He asked me if we had no such thing in my country? and I told him, No. I then asked him the use of it, and who made it; he told me a great man in the heavens, called God: but here again I was to all intents and purposes at a loss to understand him; and the more so, when a little after I saw the air filled with it, in a heavy shower, which fell down on the same day. After this I went to church; and having never been at such a place before, I was again amazed at seeing and hearing the service. I asked all I could about it; and they gave me to understand it was worshipping God, who made us and all things. I was still at a great loss, and soon got into an endless field of inquiries, as well as I was able to speak and ask about things. However, my little friend Dick used to be my best interpreter; for I could make free with him, and he always instructed me with pleasure: and from what I could understand by him of this God, and in seeing these white people did not sell one another, as we did, I was much pleased; and in this I thought they were much happier than we Africans. I was astonished at the wisdom of the white people in all things I saw; but was amazed at their not sacrificing, or making any offerings, and eating with unwashed hands, and touching the dead. I likewise could not help remarking the particular slenderness of their women, which I did not at first like; and I thought they were not so modest and shamefaced as the African women.

I had often seen my master and Dick employed in reading; and I had a great curiosity to talk to the books, as I thought they did; and so to learn how all things had a beginning: for that purpose I have often taken up a book, and have talked to it, and then put my ears to it, when alone, in hopes it would answer me; and I have been very much concerned when I found it remained silent.

My master lodged at the house of a gentleman in Falmouth, who had a fine little daughter about six or seven years of age, and she grew prodigiously fond of me; insomuch that we used to eat together, and had servants to wait on us. I was so much caressed by this family that it often reminded me of the treatment I had received from my little noble African master. After

I had been here a few days, I was sent on board of the ship; but the child cried so much after me that nothing could pacify her till I was sent for again. It is ludicrous enough, that I began to fear I should be betrothed to this young lady; and when my master asked me if I would stay there with her behind him, as he was going away with the ship, which had taken in the tobacco again? I cried immediately, and said I would not leave him. At last, by stealth, one night I was sent on board the ship again; and in a little time we sailed for Guernsey, where she was in part owned by a merchant, one Nicholas Doberry. As I was now amongst a people who had not their faces scarred, like some of the African nations where I had been, I was very glad I did not let them ornament me in that manner when I was with them. When we arrived at Guernsey, my master placed me to board and lodge with one of his mates, who had a wife and family there; and some months afterwards he went to England, and left me in the care of this mate, together with my friend Dick. This mate had a little daughter aged about five or six years, with whom I used to be much delighted. I had often observed, that when her mother washed her face it looked very rosy; but when she washed mine it did not look so; I therefore tried oftentimes myself if I could not by washing make my face of the same colour as my little play-mate (Mary), but it was all in vain; and I now began to be mortified at the difference in our complexions. This woman behaved to me with great kindness and attention; and taught me every thing in the same manner as she did her own child, and indeed in every respect treated me as such. I remained here till the summer of the year 1757, when my master, being appointed first lieutenant of His Majesty's ship the *Roebuck*, sent for Dick and me, and his old mate: on this we all left Guernsey, and set out for England in a sloop bound for London. As we were coming up towards the Nore, where the *Roebuck* lay, a man of war's boat came along-side to press our people; on which each man ran to hide himself. I was very much frightened at this, though I did not know what it meant, or what to think or do. However, I went and hid myself also under a hencoop. Immediately the press-gang came on board with their swords drawn, and searched all about, pulled the people out by force, and put them into the boat. At last I was found out also; the man that found me held me up by the heels while they all made their sport of me, I roaring and crying out all the time most lustily; but at last the mate, who was my conductor, seeing this, came to my assistance, and did all he could to pacify me; but all to very little purpose, till I had seen the boat go off. Soon afterwards we came to the Nore, where the *Roebuck* lay; and, to our great joy, my master came on board to us, and brought us to the ship. I was amazed indeed to see the quantity of men and the guns. However my surprise began to diminish, as my knowledge increased; and I ceased to feel those apprehensions and alarms which had taken such strong possession of me when I first came among the Europeans, and for some time after. I began now to pass to an opposite extreme; I was so far from being afraid of any thing new which

I saw, that, after I had been some time in this ship, I even began to long for an engagement. My griefs too, which in young minds are not perpetual, were now wearing away; and I soon enjoyed myself pretty well, and felt tolerably easy in my present situation. There was a number of boys on board, which still made it more agreeable; for we were always together, and a great part of our time was spent in play. I remained in this ship a considerable time, during which we made several cruises, and visited a variety of places: among others we were twice in Holland, and brought over several persons of distinction from it, whose names I do not now remember. On the passage, one day, for the diversion of those gentlemen, all the boys were called on the quarter-deck, and were paired proportionably, and then made to fight; after which the gentleman gave the combatants from five to nine shillings each. This was the first time I ever fought with a white boy; and I never knew what it was to have a bloody nose before. This made me fight most desperately; I suppose considerably more than an hour; and at last, both of us being weary, we were parted. I had a great deal of this kind of sport afterwards, in which the captain and the ship's company used very much to encourage me. Sometime afterwards the ship went to Leith, in Scotland, from thence to the Orkneys, where I was surprised in seeing scarcely any night; and from thence we sailed with a great fleet, full of soldiers, for England. All this time we had never come to an engagement, though we were frequently cruising off the coast of France; during which we chased many vessels, and took in all seventeen prizes. I had been learning many of the manoeuvres of the ship during our cruise; and I was several times made to fire the guns.

One evening, off Havre de Grace, just as it was growing dark, we were standing off shore, and met with a fine large French-built frigate. We got all things immediately ready for fighting; and I now expected I should be gratified in seeing an engagement, which I had so long wished for in vain. But the very moment the word of command was given to fire, we heard those on board the other ship cry 'Haul down the jib' and in that instant she hoisted English colours. There was instantly with us an amazing cry of – 'Avast!' or 'stop firing!' and I think one or two guns had been let off, but happily they did no mischief. We had hailed them several times; but they not hearing, we received no answer, which was the cause of our firing. The boat was then sent on board of her, and she proved to be the *Ambuscade* man of war, to my no small disappointment. We returned to Portsmouth, without having been in any action, just at the trial of Admiral Byng (whom I saw several times during it); and my master, having left the ship, and gone to London for promotion, Dick and I were put on board the *Savage* sloop of war, and we went in her to assist in bringing off the *St George* man of war, that had run ashore somewhere on the coast. After staying a few weeks on board the *Savage*, Dick and I were sent on shore at Deal, where we remained some short time, till my master sent for us to London, the place I had long desired exceedingly to see. We therefore both with great pleasure got into a waggon, and came to London, where we were received by a Mr Guerin, a relation of my master. This gentleman had two sisters, very amiable ladies, who took much notice and great care of me. Though I had desired so much to see London, when I arrived in it I was unfortunately unable to gratify my curiosity; for I had at this time the chilblains to such a degree that I could not stand for several months, and I was obliged to be sent to St George's Hospital. There I grew so ill, that the doctors wanted to cut my left leg off at different times, apprehending a mortification; but I always said I would rather die than suffer it; and happily (I thank God) I recovered without the operation. After being there several weeks, and just as I had recovered, the small-pox broke out on me, so that I was again confined; and I thought myself now particularly unfortunate. However, I soon recovered again: and by this time my master having been promoted to be first lieutenant of the *Preston* man of war of fifty guns, then new at Deptford, Dick and I were sent on board her, and soon we went to Holland to bring over the late Duke of Cumberland to England. While I was in this ship an incident happened, which though trifling, I beg leave to relate, as I could not help taking particular notice of it, and considering it then as a judgment of God. One morning a young man was looking up to the fore-top, and in a wicked tone, common on shipboard, d–d his eyes about something. Just at the moment some small particles of dirt fell into his left eye, and by the evening it was very much inflamed.

The next day it grew worse; and within six or seven days he lost it. From this ship my master was appointed a lieutenant on board the *Royal George*. When he was going he wished me to stay on board the Preston, to learn the French horn; but the ship being ordered for Turkey, I could not think of leaving my master, to whom I was very warmly attached; and I told him, if he left me behind it would break my heart. This prevailed on him to take me with him; but he left Dick on board the *Preston*, whom I embraced at parting for the last time. The *Royal George* was the largest ship I had ever seen; so that when I came on board of her I was surprised at the number of people, men, women, and children, of every denomination; and the largeness of the guns, many of them also of brass, which I had never seen before. Here were also shops or stalls of every kind of goods, and people crying their different commodities about the ship as in a town. To me it appeared a little world, into which I was again cast without a friend, for I had no longer my dear companion Dick. We did not stay long here. My master was not many weeks on board before he got an appointment to be sixth lieutenant of the *Namur*, which was then at Spithead, fitting up for Vice-Admiral Boscawen, who was going with a large fleet on an expedition against Louisbourgh. The crew of the *Royal George* were turned over to her, and the flag of that gallant Admiral was hoisted on board, the blue at the maintop gallant-mast head. There was a very great fleet of men of war of every description assembled together for this expedition, and I was in hopes soon to have an opportunity of being gratified with a sea-fight. All things being now in readiness, this mighty fleet (for there was also Admiral Cornish's fleet in company, destined for the East Indies) at last weighed anchor, and sailed. The two fleets continued in company for several days, and then parted; Admiral Cornish, in the *Lenox*, having first saluted our Admiral in the *Namur*, which he returned. We then steered for America; but, by contrary winds, we were driven to Teneriffe, where I was struck with its noted peak. Its prodigious height, and its form, resembling a sugar loaf, filled me with wonder. We remained in sight of this island some days, and then proceeded for America, which we soon made, and got into a very commodious harbour called St George, in Halifax, where we had fish in great plenty, and all other fresh provisions. We were here joined by different men of war and transport ships with soldiers; after which, our fleet being increased to a prodigious number of ships of all kinds, we sailed for Cape Breton in Nova Scotia. We had the good and gallant General Wolfe on board our ship, whose affability made him highly esteemed and beloved by all the men. He often honoured me, as well as other boys, with marks of his notice; and saved me once a flogging for fighting with a young gentleman. We arrived at Cape Breton in the summer of 1758: and here the soldiers were to be landed, in order to make an attack upon Louisbourgh. My master had some part in superintending the landing; and here I was in a small measure gratified in seeing an encounter between our men and the enemy. The French were posted on the shore to receive us, and disputed our landing for a long time: but at last they were driven from their trenches, and a complete landing was effected. Our troops pursued them as far as the town of Louisbourgh. In this action many were killed on both sides. One thing remarkable I saw this day; – A lieutenant of the *Princess Amelia*, who, as well as my master, superintended the landing, was giving the word of command, and while his mouth was open a musket ball went through it, and passed out at his cheek. I had that day in my hand the scalp of an Indian king, who was killed in the engagement: the scalp had been taken off by an Highlander. I saw this king's ornaments too, which were very curious, and made of feathers.

Our land forces laid siege to the town of Louisbourgh, while the French men of war were blocked up in the harbour by the fleet, the batteries at the same time playing upon them from the land. This they did with such effect, that one day I saw some of the ships set on fire by the shells from the batteries, and I believe two or three of them were quite burnt. At another time, about fifty boats belonging to the English men of war, commanded by Captain George Balfour of the *Aetna* fireship, and Mr Laforey, another junior captain, attacked and boarded the only two remaining French men of war in the harbour. They also set fire to a seventy-gun ship, but they brought off a sixty-four, called the *Bienfaisant*. During my stay here I had often an opportunity of being near Captain Balfour, who was pleased to notice me, and liked me so much that he often asked my master to let him have me, but he would not part with me; and no consideration would have induced me to leave him. At last Louisbourgh was taken, and the English men of war came into the harbour before it, to my very great joy; for I had now more liberty of indulging myself, and I went often on shore. When the ships were in the harbour, we had the most beautiful procession on the water I ever saw. All the admirals and captains of the men of war, full dressed, and in their barges, well ornamented with pendants, came alongside of the *Namur*. The Vice-admiral then went on shore in his barge, followed by the other officers in order of seniority, to take possession, as I suppose, of the town and fort. Some time after this the French governor and his lady, and other persons of note, came on board our ship to dine. On this occasion our ships were dressed with colours of all kinds, from the topgallant-mast head to the deck; and this, with the firing of guns, formed a most grand and magnificent spectacle.

As soon as every thing here was settled, Admiral Boscawen sailed with part of the fleet for England, leaving some ships behind with Rear Admirals Sir Charles Hardy and Durell. It was now winter; and one evening, during our passage home, about dusk, when we were in the channel, or near soundings and were beginning to look for land, we descried seven sail of large men of war, which stood off shore. Several people on board of our ship said, as the two fleets were (in forty minutes from the first sight) within hail of each other, that they were English men of war; and some of our people even began to name some of the ships. By this time both fleets began to mingle, and our admiral ordered his flag to be hoisted. At that instant, the other fleet, which were French, hoisted their ensigns, and gave us a broadside as they passed by. Nothing could create greater surprise and confusion among us than this. The wind was high, the sea rough, and we had our lower and middle deck guns housed in, so that not a single gun on board was ready to be fired at any of the French ships. However, the *Royal William* and the *Somerset*, being our sternmost ships, became a little prepared, and each gave the French ships a broadside as they passed by. I afterwards heard this was a French squadron, commanded by Mons. Conflans; and certainly had the Frenchman known our condition, and had a mind to fight us, they might have done us great mischief. But we were not long before we were prepared for an engagement. Immediately many things were tossed overboard; the ships were made ready for fighting as soon as possible; and about ten at night we had bent a new main sail, the old one being split. Being now in readiness for fighting, we wore ship, and stood after the French fleet, who were one or two ships in number more than we. However, we gave them chase, and continued pursuing them all night; and at day-light we saw six of them, all large ships of the line, and an English East-Indiaman, a prize they had taken. We chased them all day till between three and four o'clock in the evening, when we came up with, and passed within a musquet shot of one seventy-four gun ship and the Indiaman also, who now hoisted her colours, but immediately hauled them down again. On this we

made a signal for the other ships to take possession of
her; and, supposing the man of war would likewise
strike, we cheered, but she did not; though if we had
fired into her, from being so near, we must have taken
her. To my utter surprise the *Somerset*, who was the
next ship a-stern of the *Namur*, made way likewise;
and, thinking they were sure of this French ship, they
cheered in the same manner, but still continued to
follow us. The French Commodore was about a gun-
shot a-head of all, running from us with all speed;
and about four o'clock he carried his fore-top-mast
overboard. This caused another loud cheer with us;
and a little after the top-mast came close by us; but, to
our great surprise, instead of coming up with her, we
found she went as fast as ever, if not faster. The sea
grew now much smoother; and the wind lulling, the
seventy-four gun ship we had passed came again by us
in the very same direction, and so near, that we heard
her people talk as she went by; yet not a shot was fired
on either side; and about five or six o'clock, just as it
grew dark, she joined her Commodore. We chased all
night; but the next day they were out of sight, so that
we saw no more of them; and we only had the old
Indiaman (called *Carnarvon* I think) for our trouble.
After this, we stood in for the channel, and soon made
the land; and, about the close of the year 1758–9, we
got safe to St Helen's. Here the *Namur* ran a-ground;
and also another large ship a-stern of us; but, by start-
ing our water, and tossing many things overboard to
lighten her, we got the ships off without any damage.
We stayed for a short time at Spithead, and then went

into Portsmouth harbour to refit; from whence the Admiral went to London; and my master and I soon followed, with a press-gang, as we wanted some hands to complete our complement.

4. The Englishman

It was now between three and four years since I first came to England, a great part of which I had spent at sea; so that I became inured to that service, and began to consider myself as happily situated; for my master treated me always extremely well; and my attachment and gratitude to him were very great. From the various scenes I had beheld on ship-board, I soon grew a stranger to terror of every kind, and was, in that respect at least, almost an Englishman. I have often reflected with surprise that I never felt half the alarm at any of the numerous dangers I have been in, that I was filled with at the first sight of the Europeans, and at every act of theirs, even the most trifling, when I first came among them, and for some time afterwards. That fear, however, which was the effect of my ignorance, wore away as I began to know them. I could now speak English tolerably well, and I perfectly understood every thing that was said. I now not only felt myself quite easy with these new countrymen, but relished their society and manners. I no longer looked upon them as spirits, but as men superior to us; and therefore I had the stronger desire to resemble them; to imbibe their spirit, and imitate their manners; I therefore embraced every occasion of improvement; and every new thing that I observed I treasured up in my memory. I had long wished to be able to read and write; and for this purpose I took every opportunity to gain instruction, but had made as yet very little progress. However, when I went to London with my master, I had soon an opportunity of improving myself, which I gladly embraced. Shortly after my arrival, he sent me to wait upon the Miss Guerins, who had treated me with much kindness when I was there before; and they sent me to school.

While I was attending these ladies, their servants told me I could not go to heaven, unless I was baptized. This made me very uneasy; for I had now some faint idea of a future state: accordingly I communicated my anxiety to the eldest Miss Guerin, with whom I was become a favourite, and pressed her to have me baptized; when, to my great joy, she told me I should. She had formerly asked my master to let me be baptized, but he had refused; however, she now insisted on it; and he, being under some obligation to her brother, complied with her request; so I was baptized at St Margaret's church, Westminster, in February 1759, by my present name. The clergyman, at the same time, gave me a book, called a guide to the Indians, written by the Bishop of Sodor and Man. On this occasion, Miss Guerin and her brother did me the honour to stand as godfather and godmother, and afterwards gave me a treat. I used to attend these ladies about the town, in which service I was extremely happy; as I had thus very much opportunities of seeing London, which I desired of all things. I was sometimes, however, with my master at his rendezvous-house, which was at the foot of Westminster bridge. Here I used to enjoy myself in playing about the bridge stairs, and often in the watermen's wherries with other boys. On one of these occasions there was another boy with me in a wherry, and we went out into the current of the river; while there, two more stout boys came to us in another wherry, and, abusing us for taking the boat, desired me to get into the other wherry-boat. Accordingly I went to get out of the wherry I was in; but just as I had got one of my feet into the other boat, the boys shoved it off, so that I fell into the Thames and, not being able to swim, I should unavoidably have been drowned, but for the assistance of some watermen, who providentially came to my relief.

The *Namur* being again got ready for sea, my master, with his gang, was ordered on board; and, to my no small grief, I was obliged to leave my school-master, whom I liked very much, and always attended while I stayed in London, to repair on board with my master. Nor did I leave my kind patronesses, the Miss Guerins, without uneasiness and regret. They often used to teach me to read, and took great pains to instruct me in the principles of religion, and the knowledge of God. I therefore parted from those amiable ladies with reluctance; after receiving from them many friendly cautions how to conduct myself, and some valuable presents.

When I came to Spithead, I found we were destined for the Mediterranean, with a large fleet, which was now ready to put to sea. We only waited for the arrival of the admiral, who soon came on board; and about the beginning of the spring 1759, having weighed anchor and got under way, sailed for the Mediter-ranean; and in eleven days from the Land's End, we got to Gibraltar. While we were here I used to be often on shore, and got various fruits in great plenty, and very cheap.

I had frequently told several people, in my excursions on shore, the story of my being kidnapped with my sister, and of our being separated, as I have related before; and I had as often expressed my anxiety for her fate, and my sorrow at having never met her again. One day, when I was on shore, and mentioning these circumstances to some persons, one of them told me he knew where my sister was, and if I would accompany him, he would bring me to her. Improbable as this story was, I believed it immediately, and agreed to go with him, while my heart leaped for joy; and, indeed, he conducted me to a black young woman, who was so like my sister that, at first sight, I really thought it was she; but I was quickly undeceived; and, on talking to her, I found her to be of another nation.

While we lay here the *Preston* came in from the Levant. As soon as she arrived, my master told me I should now see my old companion Dick, who was gone in her when she sailed for Turkey. I was much rejoiced at this information, and expected every minute to embrace him; and when the captain came on board of our ship, which he did immediately after, I ran to enquire about my friend; but, with inexpressible sorrow, I learned from the boat's crew that the dear youth was dead! and that they had brought his chest, and all his other things to my master: these he afterwards gave to me, and I regarded them as a memorial of my friend, whom I loved and grieved for as a brother.

While we were at Gibraltar I saw a soldier hanging by the heels at one of the moles. I thought this a strange sight, as I had seen a man hanged in London by his neck. At another time I saw the master of a frigate towed to shore on a grating, by several of the men of war's boats, and discharged the fleet, which I understood was a mark of disgrace for cowardice. On board the same ship a sailor was also hung up at the main-yard-arm.

After lying at Gibraltar for some time, we sailed up the Mediterranean, a considerable way above the gulf of Lyons: where we were one night overtaken by a terrible gale of wind, much greater than any I had ever yet experienced. The sea ran so high that, though all the guns were well housed, there was great reason to fear their getting loose, the ship rolled so much; and if they had, it must have proved our destruction. After we had cruised here for a short time, we came to Barcelona, a Spanish sea-port, remarkable for its silk manufactories. Here the ships were all to be watered; and my master, who spoke different languages, and used often to interpret for the admiral, superintended the watering of ours. For that purpose he and the officers of the other ships, who were on the same service, had tents pitched in the bay; and the Spanish soldiers were stationed along the shore, I suppose to see that no depredations were committed by our men.

I used constantly to attend my master, and I was charmed with this place. All the time of our stay it was

like a fair with the natives, who brought us fruits of all
kinds, and sold them to us much cheaper than I had
got them in England. They used also to bring wine
down to us in hog and sheep skins, which diverted
me very much. The Spanish officers here treated our
officers with great politeness and attention; and some
of them, in particular, used to come often to my
master's tent to visit him; where they did sometimes
divert themselves by mounting me on the horses or
mules, so that I could not fall, and setting them off at
full gallop; my imperfect skill in horsemanship all the
while affording them no small entertainment. After
the ships were watered, we returned to our old station
of cruizing off Toulon, for the purpose of intercepting
a fleet of French men of war that lay there. One
Sunday, in our cruize, we came off a place where there
were two small French frigates lying in shore; and our
admiral, thinking to take or destroy them, sent two
ships in after them – the *Culloden* and the *Conqueror*.
They soon came up to the Frenchmen, and I saw a
smart fight here, both by sea and land: for the frigates
were covered by batteries, and they played upon our
ships most furiously, which they as furiously returned,
and for a long time a constant firing was kept up, on
all sides, at an amazing rate. At last one frigate sunk;
but the people escaped, though not without much
difficulty: and a little after some of the people left the
other frigate also, which was a mere wreck. However,
our ships did not venture to bring her away, they were
so much annoyed from the batteries, which raked them
both in going and coming; their top-masts were shot

away, and they were otherwise so much shattered, that the admiral was obliged to send in many boats to tow them back to the fleet. I afterwards sailed with a man who fought in one of the French batteries during the engagement, and he told me our ships had done considerable mischief that day on shore, and in the batteries.

After this we sailed for Gibraltar, and arrived there about August 1759. Here we remained with all our sails unbent, while the fleet was watering and doing other necessary things. While we were in this situation, one day the admiral, with most of the principal officers, and many people of all stations, being on shore, about seven o'clock in the evening we were alarmed by signals from the frigates stationed for that purpose; and in an instant there was a general cry that the French fleet was out, and just passing through the streights. The admiral immediately came on board with some other officers; and it is impossible to describe the noise, hurry, and confusion, throughout the whole fleet, in bending their sails, and slipping their cables; many people and ship's boats were left on shore in the bustle. We had two captains on board of our ship, who came away in the hurry and left their ships to follow. We shewed lights from the gun-wales to the main-top-mast-head; and all our lieutenants were employed amongst the fleet to tell the ships not to wait for their captains, but to put the sails to the yards, slip their cables and follow us; and in this confusion of making ready for fighting, we set out for sea in the dark after the French fleet.

They had got the start of us so far that we were not

able to come up with them during the night; but at day-light we saw seven sail of ships of the line some miles a-head. We immediately chased them till about four o'clock in the evening, when our ships came up with them; and though we were about fifteen large ships, our gallant admiral only fought them with his own division, which consisted of seven; so that we were just ship for ship. We passed by the whole of the enemy's fleet in order to come at their commander, Mons. La Clue, who was in the *Ocean*, an eighty-four gun ship: as we passed they all fired on us; and at one time three of them fired together, continuing to do so for some time. Notwithstanding which our admiral would not suffer a gun to be fired at any of them, to my astonishment; but made us lie on our bellies on the deck till we came quite close to the *Ocean*, who was a-head of them all; when we had orders to pour the whole three tiers into her at once.

The engagement now commenced with great fury on both sides: the *Ocean* immediately returned our fire, and we continued engaged with each other for some time; during which I was frequently stunned with the thundering of the great guns, whose dreadful contents hurried many of my companions into awful eternity. At last the French line was entirely broken, and we obtained the victory, which was immediately pro-claimed with loud huzzas and acclamations. We took three prizes, *La Modeste*, of sixty-four guns, and *Le Temeraire* and *Centaur*, of seventy-four guns each. The rest of the French ships took to flight with all the sail they could crowd. Our ship being very much damaged, and quite disabled from pursuing the enemy, the admiral immediately quitted her, and went in the broken, and only boat we had left, on board the *Newark*, with which, and some other ships, he went after the French. The *Ocean*, and another large French ship, called the *Redoutable*, endeavouring to escape, ran ashore at Cape Logas, on the coast of Portugal; and the French admiral and some of the crew got ashore; but we, finding it impossible to get the ships off, set fire to them both. About midnight I saw the *Ocean* blow up, with a most dreadful explosion. I never beheld a more awful scene. About the space of a minute, the midnight seemed turned into day by the blaze, which was attended with a noise louder and more terrible than thunder, that seemed to rend every element around us.

My station during the engagement was on the middle deck, where I was quartered with another boy, to bring powder to the aftermost gun; and here I was a witness of the dreadful fate of many of my companions, who, in the twinkling of an eye, were dashed in pieces, and launched into eternity. Happily I escaped unhurt, though the shot and splinters flew thick about me during the whole fight. Towards the latter part of it my master was wounded, and I saw him carried down to the surgeon; but, though I was much alarmed for him, and wished to assist him, I dared not leave my post. At this station my gun-mate (a partner in bringing powder for the same gun) and I ran a very great risk for more than half an hour of blowing up the ship. For, when we had taken the cartridges out of the boxes, the bottoms of many of them proving rotten, the powder ran all about the deck, near the match-tub: we scarcely had water enough at the last to throw on it. We were also, from our employment, very much exposed to the enemy's shots; for we had to go through nearly the whole length of the ship to bring the powder. I expected therefore every minute to be my last; especially when I saw our men fall so thick about me; but, wishing to guard as much against the dangers as possible, at first I thought it would be safest not to go for the powder till the Frenchmen had fired their broadside; and then, while they were charging, I could go and come with my powder: but immediately afterwards I thought this caution was fruitless; and, cheering myself with the reflection that there was a time allotted for me to die as well as to be born, I instantly cast off all fear or thought whatever of death, and went through the whole of my duty with alacrity; pleasing myself with the hope, if I survived the battle, of relating it and the dangers I had escaped to the Miss Guerins, and others, when I should return to London.

Our ship suffered very much in this engagement; for, besides the number of our killed and wounded, she was almost torn to pieces, and our rigging so much shattered, that our mizen-mast, main-yard, &c. hung over the side of the ship; so that we were obliged to get many carpenters and others, from some of the ships of the fleet, to assist in setting us in some tolerable order; and, notwithstanding which, it took us some time before we were completely refitted; after which we left Admiral Broderick to command, and we, with the prizes, steered for England. On the passage, and as soon as my master was something recovered of his wounds, the Admiral appointed him captain of the *Aetna* fire-ship, on which he and I left the *Namur*, and went on board of her at sea. I liked this small ship very much. I now became the captain's steward, in which situation I was very happy, for I was extremely well treated by all on board, and I had leisure to improve myself in reading and writing. The latter I had learned a little before I left the *Namur*, as there was a school on board. When we arrived at Spithead, the Aetna went into Portsmouth harbour to refit, which being done, we returned to Spithead, and joined a large fleet that was thought to be intended against the *Havannah*. But about that time the king died; whether that prevented the expedition I know not; but it caused our ship to be stationed at Cowes, in the Isle of Wight, till the beginning of the year sixty-one. Here I spent my time very pleasantly; I was much on shore all about this delightful island, and found the inhabitants very civil.

While I was here, I met with a trifling incident which surprised me agreeably. I was one day in a field belonging to a gentleman who had a black boy about my own size; this boy having observed me from his master's house, was transported at the sight of one of his own countrymen, and ran to meet me with the utmost haste. I not knowing what he was about, turned a little out of his way at first, but to no purpose; he soon came close to me, and caught hold of me in his arms as if I had been his brother, though we had never seen each other before. After we had talked together for some time, he took me to his master's house, where I was treated very kindly. This benevolent boy and I were very happy in frequently seeing each other, till about the month of March 1761, when our ship had orders to fit out again for another expedition. When we got ready, we joined a very large fleet at Spithead, commanded by Commodore Keppel, destined against Belle-Isle; and having a number of transport ships in company, with troops on board, to make a descent on the place, we sailed once more in quest of fame. I longed to engage in new adventures, and to see fresh wonders.

I had a mind on which every thing uncommon made its full impression, and every event which I considered as marvellous. Every extraordinary escape, or signal deliverance, either of myself or others, I looked upon to be effected by the interposition of Providence. We had not been above ten days at sea before an incident of this kind happened; which, whatever credit it may obtain from the reader, made no small impression upon my mind.

We had on board a gunner, whose name was John Mondle, a man of very indifferent morals. This man's cabin was between the decks, exactly over where I lay, a-breast of the quarter-deck ladder. One night, the 5th of April, being terrified with a dream, he awoke in so great a fright that he could not rest in his bed any longer, nor even remain in his cabin; and he went upon deck about four o'clock in the morning extremely agitated. He immediately told those upon the deck of the agonies of his mind, and the dream which occasioned it; in which he said he had seen many things very awful, and had been warned by St Peter to repent, who told him his time was short. This he said had greatly alarmed him, and he was determined to alter his life. People generally mock the fears of others when they are themselves in safety; and some of his shipmates who heard him only laughed at him. However, he made a vow that he never would drink strong liquors again; and he immediately got a light, and gave away his sea-stores of liquor. After which, his agitation still continuing, he began to read the scriptures, hoping to find some relief; and soon afterwards he laid himself down again on his bed, and endeavoured to compose himself to sleep, but to no purpose; his mind still continuing in a state of agony. By this time it was exactly half after seven in the morning; I was then under the half deck at the great cabin door; and all at once I heard the people in the waist cry out most fearfully – 'The Lord have mercy upon us! We are all lost! The Lord have mercy upon us!' – Mr Mondle hearing the cries, immediately ran out of his cabin; and we were instantly struck by the *Lynne*, a forty-gun ship, Captain Clerk, which nearly ran us down. This ship had just put about, and was by the wind, but had not got full head-way, or we must all have perished; for the wind was brisk. However, before Mr Mondle had got four steps from his cabin door, she struck our ship, with her cutwater, right in the middle of his bed and cabin, and ran it up to the combings of the quarter deck hatchway, and above three feet below water, and in a minute there was not a bit of wood to be seen where Mr Mondle's cabin stood; and he was so near being killed, that some of the splinters tore his face. As Mr Mondle must inevitably have perished from this accident, had he not been alarmed in the very extraordinary way I have related, I could not help regarding this as an awful interposition of Providence for his preservation. The two ships for some time swinged alongside of each other; for ours being a fireship, our grappling-irons caught the *Lynne* every way, and the yards and rigging went at an astonishing rate. Our ship was in such a shocking condition that we all thought she would instantly go down, and every one ran for their lives, and got as well as they could on board the *Lynne*; but our lieutenant being the aggressor, he never quitted the ship. However, when we found she did not sink, immediately, the captain came on board again and encouraged our people to return and try to save her. Many of them came back, but some would not venture. Some of the ships in the fleet, seeing our situation, immediately sent their boats to our assistance; but it took us the whole day to save the ship with all their help. And by using every possible means, particularly frapping her together with many hawsers, and putting a great quantity of tallow below water where she was damaged, she was kept together; but it was well we did not meet with any gales of wind, or we must have gone to pieces; for we were in such a crazy condition that we had ships to attend us till we arrived at Belle-Isle, the place of our destination; and then we had all things taken out of the ship, and she was properly repaired. This escape of Mr Mondle, which he, as well as myself, always considered as a singular act of Providence, I believe had a great influence on his life and conduct ever afterwards.

Now that I am on this subject, I beg leave to relate another instance or two which strongly raised my belief of the particular interposition of Heaven, and which might not otherwise have found a place here, from their insignificance. I belonged for a few days, in the year 1758, to the *Jason*, of fifty-four guns, at Plymouth; and one night, when I was on board, a woman, with a child at her breast, fell from the upper deck down into the hold, near the keel. Every one thought that the mother and child must be both dashed to pieces; but, to our great surprise, neither of them was hurt. I myself one day fell headlong from the upper deck of the *Aetna* down the after-hold, when the ballast was out; and all who saw me fall called out I was killed; but I received not the least injury. And in the same ship a man fell from the mast-head on the deck without being hurt. In these, and in many more instances, I thought I could very plainly trace the hand of God, without whose permission a sparrow cannot fall. I began to raise my fear from man to him alone, and to call daily on his holy name with fear and reverence: and I trust he heard my supplications, and graciously condescended to answer me according to his holy word, and to implant the seeds of piety in me, even one of the meanest of his creatures.

When we had refitted our ship, and all things were in readiness for attacking the place, the troops on board the transports were ordered to disembark; and my master, as a junior captain, had a share in the command of the landing. This was on the 12th of April. The French were drawn up on the shore, and had made every disposition to oppose the landing of our men, only a small part of them this day being able to effect it; most of them, after fighting with great bravery, were cut off, and General Crawford, with a number of others, were taken prisoners. In this day's engagement we had also our lieutenant killed.

On the 21st of April we renewed our efforts to land the men, while all the men of war were stationed along the shore to cover it, and fired at the French batteries and breastworks, from early in the morning till about four o'clock in the evening, when our soldiers effected a safe landing. They immediately attacked the French; and, after a sharp encounter, forced them from the batteries. Before the enemy retreated, they blew up several of them, lest they should fall into our hands. Our men then proceeded to besiege the citadel, and my master was ordered on shore to superintend the landing of all the materials necessary for carrying on the siege; in this service I mostly attended him. While I was there I went about to different parts of the island; and one day, particularly, my curiosity almost cost me my life. I wanted very much to see the mode of charging the mortars, and letting off the shells, and for that purpose I went to an English battery that was but a very few yards from the walls of the citadel. There indeed I had an opportunity of completely gratifying myself in seeing the whole operation, and that not without running a very great risk, both from the

English shells that burst while I was there, but likewise from those of the French. One of the largest of their shells bursted within nine or ten yards of me: there was a single rock close by, about the size of a butt; and I got instant shelter under it in time to avoid the fury of the shell. Where it burst the earth was torn in such a manner that two or three butts might easily have gone into the hole it made, and it threw great quantities of stones and dirt to a considerable distance. Three shot were also fired at me, and another boy who was along with me, one of them in particular seemed

Wing'd with red lightning and impetuous rage;

for, with a most dreadful sound, it hissed close by me, and struck a rock at a little distance, which it shattered to pieces. When I saw what perilous circumstances I was in, I attempted to return the nearest way I could find, and thereby I got between the English and the French centinels. An English serjeant, who commanded the outposts, seeing me, and surprised how I came there (which was by stealth along the sea-shore), reprimanded me very severely for it, and instantly took the centinel off his post into custody, for his negligence in suffering me to pass the lines. While I was in this situation I observed at a little distance a French horse belonging to some islanders, which I thought I would now mount, for the greater expedition of getting off. Accordingly, I took some cord which I had about me, and making a kind of bridle of it, I put it round the horse's head, and the tame beast very quietly suffered me to tie him thus and mount him. As soon as I was on the horse's back I began to kick and beat him, and try every means to make him go quick, but all to very little purpose: I could not drive him out of a slow pace. While I was creeping along, still within reach of the enemy's shot, I met with a servant well mounted on an English horse. I immediately stopped; and, crying, told him my case; and begged of him to help me, and this he effectually did; for, having a fine large whip, he began to lash my horse with it so severely, that he set off full speed with me towards the sea, while I was quite unable to hold or manage him. In this manner I went along till I came to a craggy precipice. I now could not stop my horse; and my mind was filled with apprehensions of my deplorable fate, should he go down the precipice, which he appeared fully disposed to do: I therefore thought I had better throw myself off him at once, which I did immediately with a great deal of dexterity, and fortunately escaped unhurt. As soon as I found myself at liberty, I made the best of my way for the ship, determined I would not be so fool-hardy again in a hurry.

We continued to besiege the citadel till June, when it surrendered. During the siege I have counted above sixty shells and carcases in the air at once. When this place was taken I went through the citadel, and in the bomb-proofs under it, which were cut in the solid rock; and I thought it a surprising place both for strength and building: notwithstanding which our shots and shells had made amazing devastation, and ruinous heaps all around it.

After the taking of this island, our ships, with some others commanded by Commodore Stanhope, in the *Swiftsure*, went to Basse-road, where we blocked up a French fleet. Our ships were there from June till February following; and in that time I saw a great many scenes of war, and stratagems on both sides, to destroy each other's fleet. Sometimes we would attack the French with some ships of the line; at other times with boats; and frequently we made prizes. Once or twice the French attacked us, by throwing shells with their bomb-vessels; and one day, as a French vessel was throwing shells at our ships, she broke from her springs behind the Isle of Rhe: the tide being complicated, she came within a gun-shot of the *Nassau*; but the *Nassau* could not bring a gun to bear upon her, and thereby the Frenchman got off. We were twice attacked by their fire-floats, which they chained together, and then let them float down with the tide; but each time we sent boats with grapplings, and towed them safe out of the fleet.

We had different commanders while we were at this place, Commodores Stanhope, Dennis, Lord Howe, &c. From thence, before the Spanish war began, our ship and, the *Wasp* sloop, were sent to St Sebastian, in Spain, by Commodore Stanhope; and Commodore Dennis afterwards sent our ship as a cartel to Bayonne in France; after which we went in February 1762, to Belle-Isle, and there stayed till the summer, then we left it, and returned to Portsmouth.

After our ship was fitted out again for service, in September she went to Guernsey, where I was very glad to see my old hostess, who was now a widow, and my former little charming companion her daughter. I spent some time here very happily with them, till October, when we had orders to repair to Portsmouth. We parted from each other with a great deal of affection, and I promised to return soon, and see them again, not knowing what all-powerful fate had determined for me. Our ship having arrived at Portsmouth, we went into the harbour, and remained there till the end of November, when we heard great talk about peace; and, to our very great joy, in the beginning of December we had orders to go up to London with our ship, to be paid off. We received this news with loud huzzas, and every other demonstration of gladness; and nothing but mirth was to be seen through every part of the ship. I too was not without my share of the general joy on this occasion. I thought now of nothing but being freed, and working for myself, and thereby getting money to enable me to get a good education; for I always had a great desire to be able at least to read and write; and while I was on ship-board I had endeavoured to improve myself in both. While I was in the *Aetna* particularly, the captain's clerk taught me to write, and gave me a smattering of arithmetic as far as the rule of three. There was also one Daniel Queen, about forty years of age, a man very well educated, who messed with me on board this ship, and he likewise dressed and attended the captain. Fortunately this man soon became very much attached to me, and took very great pains to instruct me in many things. He taught me to shave and dress hair a little, and also to read in the Bible, explaining many passages to me, which I did not comprehend. I was wonderfully surprised to see the laws and rules of my country written almost exactly here; a circumstance which I believe tended to impress our manners and customs more deeply on my memory. I used to tell him of this resemblance; and many a time we had sat up the whole night together at this employment. In short he was like a father to me; and some even used to call me after his name; they also styled me the black Christian. Indeed I almost loved him with the affection of a son. Many things I have denied myself that he might have them; and when I used to play at marbles, or any other game, and won a few halfpence, or got any little money, which I did sometimes, for shaving any one, I used to buy him a little sugar or tobacco, as far as my stock of money would go. He used to say, that he and I never should part; and that when our ship was paid off, as I was as free as himself or any other man on board, he would instruct me in his business, by which I might gain a good livelihood. This gave me new life and spirits, and my heart burned within me, while I thought the time long till I obtained my freedom: for though my master had not promised it to me, yet besides the assurances I had received that he had no right to detain me, he always treated me with the greatest kindness, and reposed in me an unbounded confidence; he even paid attention to my morals; and would never suffer me to deceive him, or tell lies, of which he used to tell me the consequences; and that if I did so, God would not love me; so that from all this tenderness, I had never once supposed, in all my dreams of freedom, that he would think of detaining me any longer than I wished.

In pursuance of our orders we sailed from Portsmouth for the Thames, and arrived at Deptford the 10th of December; where we cast anchor just as it was high water. The ship was up about half an hour, when my master ordered the barge to be manned; and all in an instant, without having before given me the least reason to suspect any thing of the matter, he forced me into the barge, saying, I was going to leave him, but he would take care I should not. I was so struck with the unexpectedness of this proceeding, that for some time I could not make a reply, only I made an offer to go for my books and chest of clothes, but he swore I should not move out of his sight; and if I did he would cut my throat, at the same time taking his hanger. I began, however, to collect myself: and, plucking up courage, I told him I was free, and he could not by law serve me so. But this only enraged him the more; and he continued to swear, and said he would soon let me know whether he would or not, and at that instant sprung himself into the barge from the ship, to the astonishment and sorrow of all on board. The tide, rather unluckily for me, had just turned downward, so that we quickly fell down the river along with it, till we came among some outward-bound West-Indiamen; for he was resolved to put me on board the first vessel he could get to receive me. The boat's crew, who pulled against their will, became quite faint at different times, and would have gone ashore; but he would not let them. Some of them strove then to cheer me, and told me he could not sell me, and that they would stand by me, which revived me a little, and encouraged my hopes; for as they pulled along he asked some vessels to receive me, and they would not. But, just as we had got a little below Gravesend, we came alongside of a ship which was going away the next tide for the West Indies; her name was the *Charming Sally*, Capt. James Doran; and my master went on board and agreed with him for me; and in a little time I was sent for into the cabin. When I came there, Captain Doran asked me if I knew him. I answered that I did not; 'Then,' said he, 'you are now my slave.' I told him my master could not sell me to him, nor to any one else. 'Why,' said he, 'did not your master buy you?' I confessed he did. But I have served him, said I, many years, and he has taken all my wages and prize-money, for I only got one sixpence during the war; besides this I have been baptized; and by the laws of the land no man has a right to sell me: and I added, that I had heard a lawyer, and others at different times, tell my master so. They both then said that those people who told me so were not my friends: but I replied – It was very extraordinary that other people did not know the law as well as they. Upon this Captain Doran said I talked too much English; and if I did not behave myself well, and be quiet, he had a method on board to make me. I was too well convinced of his power over me to doubt what he said: and my former sufferings in the slave-ship presenting themselves to my mind, the recollection of them made me shudder. However, before I retired, I told them that as I could not get any right among men here, I hoped I should hereafter in Heaven; and I immediately left the cabin, filled with resentment and sorrow. The only coat I had with me my master took away with him, and said, 'If your prize-money had been £10,000 I had a right to it all, and would have taken it.' I had about nine guineas, which during my long sea-faring life, I had scraped together from trifling perquisites and little ventures; and I hid it that instant, lest my master should take that from me likewise, still hoping that by some means or other I should make my escape to the shore, and indeed some of my old shipmates told me not to despair, for they would get me back again; and that, as soon as they could get their pay, they would immediately come to Portsmouth to me, where this ship was going: but, alas! all my hopes were baffled, and the hour of my deliverance was yet far off. My master, having soon concluded his bargain with the captain, came out of the cabin, and he and his people got into the boat, and put off; I followed them with aching eyes as long as I could, and when they were out of sight I threw myself on the deck, with a heart ready to burst with sorrow and anguish.

5. Prisoner on Board

Thus, at the moment I expected all my toils to end, was I plunged, as I supposed, in a new slavery: in comparison of which all my service hitherto had been perfect freedom; and whose horrors, always present to my mind, now rushed on it with tenfold aggravation. I wept very bitterly for some time: and began to think that I must have done something to displease the Lord, that he thus punished me so severely. This filled me with painful reflections on my past conduct; I recollected that on the morning of our arrival at Deptford I had rashly sworn that as soon as we reached London I would spend the day in rambling and sport. My conscience smote me for this unguarded expression: I felt that the Lord was able to disappoint me in all things, and immediately considered my present situation as a judgment of Heaven on account of my presumption in swearing: I therefore, with contrition of heart, acknowledged my transgression to God, and poured out my soul before him with unfeigned repentance, and with earnest supplications I besought him not to abandon me in my distress, nor cast me from his mercy for ever. In a little time my grief, spent with its own violence, began to subside; and after the first confusion of my thoughts was over, I reflected with more calmness on my present condition: I considered that trials and disappointments are sometimes for our good, and I thought God might perhaps have permitted this in order to teach me wisdom and resignation; for he had hitherto shadowed me with the wings of his mercy, and by his invisible but powerful hand brought me the way I knew not. These reflections gave me a little comfort, and I rose at last from the deck with dejection and sorrow in my countenance, yet mixed with some faint hope that the *Lord would appear* for my deliverance.

Soon afterwards, as my new master was going ashore, he called me to him, and told me to behave myself well, and do the business of the ship the same as any of the rest of the boys, and that I should fare the better for it; but I made him no answer. I was then asked if I could swim, and I said, No. However I was made to go under the deck, and was well watched. The next tide the ship got under way, and soon after arrived at the Mother Bank, Portsmouth; where she waited a few days for some of the West India convoy. While I was here I tried every means I could devise among the people of the ship to get me a boat from the shore, as there was none suffered to come along side of the ship; and their own, whenever it was used, was hoisted in again immediately. A sailor on board took a guinea from me on pretence of getting me a boat; and promised me, time after time, that it was hourly to come off. When he had the watch upon deck I watched also; and looked long enough, but all in vain; I could never see either the boat or my guinea again. And what I thought was still the worst of all, the fellow gave

information, as I afterwards found, all the while to the
mates of my intention to go off, if I could in any way
do it; but, rogue-like, he never told them he had got a
guinea from me to procure my escape. However, after
we had sailed, and his trick was made known to the
ship's crew, I had some satisfaction in seeing him
detested and despised by them all for his behaviour to
me. I was still in hopes that my old shipmates would
not forget their promise to come for me to Portsmouth;
and they did at last, but not till the day before we
sailed, some of them did come there, and sent me off
some oranges, and other tokens of their regard. They
also sent me word they would come off to me themselves the next day or the day after; and a lady also,
who lived in Gosport, wrote to me that she would
come and take me out of the ship at the same time.
This lady had been once very intimate with my former
master; I used to sell and take care of a great deal of
property for her in different ships; and in return she
always shewed great friendship for me; and used to tell
my master that she would take me away to live with
her: but unfortunately for me, a disagreement soon
afterwards took place between them; and she was succeeded in my master's good graces by another lady,
who appeared sole mistress of the *Aetna*, and mostly
lodged on board. I was not so great a favourite with
this lady as with the former; she had conceived a pique
against me on some occasion when she was on board,
and she did not fail to instigate my master to treat me
in the manner he did.

However the next morning, the 30th of December,

the wind being brisk and easterly, the *Aeolus* frigate, which was to escort the convoy, made a signal for sailing. All the ships then got up their anchors; and, before any of my friends had an opportunity to come off to my relief, to my inexpressible anguish, our ship had got under way. What tumultuous emotions agitated my soul when the convoy got under sail, and I, a prisoner on board, now without hope! I kept my swimming eyes upon the land in a state of unutterable grief; not knowing what to do, and despairing how to help myself. While my mind was in this situation, the fleet sailed on, and in one day's time I lost sight of the wished-for land. In the first expressions of my grief I reproached my fate, and wished I had never been born. I was ready to curse the tide that bore us, the gale that wafted my prison, and even the ship that conducted us; and I called on death to relieve me from the horrors I felt and dreaded.

The turbulence of my emotions, however, naturally gave way to calmer thoughts, and I soon perceived what fate had decreed no mortal on earth could prevent. The convoy sailed on without any accident, with a pleasant gale and smooth sea, for six weeks, till February, when one morning the *Aeolus* ran down a brig, one of the convoy, and she instantly went down and was ingulfed in the dark recesses of the ocean. The convoy was immediately thrown into great confusion till it was day-light; and the *Aeolus* was illuminated with lights to prevent any farther mischief. On the 13th of February 1763, from the mast-head, we descried our destined island Montserrat; and soon after I beheld those

Regions of sorrow, doleful shades, where peace
And rest can rarely dwell. Hope never comes
That comes to all, but torture without end
Still urges.

At the sight of this land of bondage, a fresh horror ran
through all my frame, and chilled me to the heart. My
former slavery now rose in dreadful review to my mind,
and displayed nothing but misery, stripes, and chains;
and, in the first paroxysm of my grief, I called upon
God's thunder, and his avenging power, to direct the
stroke of death to me, rather than permit me to become
a slave, and to be sold from lord to lord.

In this state of my mind our ship came to an anchor,
and soon after discharged her cargo. I now knew what
it was to work hard; I was made to help to unload and
load the ship. And, to comfort me in my distress in
that time, two of the sailors robbed me of all my money,
and ran away from the ship. I had been so long used
to an European climate that at first I felt the scorching
West-India sun very painful, while the dashing surf
would toss the boat and the people in it frequently
above high-water mark. Sometimes our limbs were
broken with this, or even attended with instant death,
and I was day by day mangled and torn.

About the middle of May, when the ship was got
ready to sail for England, I all the time believing that
Fate's blackest clouds were gathering over my head,
and expecting their bursting would mix me with the
dead, Captain Doran sent for me ashore one morning,
and I was told by the messenger that my fate was then

determined. With trembling steps and fluttering heart
I came to the captain, and found with him one Mr
Robert King, a quaker and the first merchant in the
place. The captain then told me my former master had
sent me there to be sold; but that he had desired him
to get me the best master he could, as he told him I
was a very deserving boy, which Captain Doran said
he found to be true, and if he were to stay in the West
Indies he would be glad to keep me himself; but he
could not venture to take me to London, for he was
very sure that when I came there I would leave him. I
at that instant burst out a crying, and begged much of
him to take me to England with him, but all to no
purpose. He told me he had got me the very best
master in the whole island, with whom I should be as
happy as if I were in England, and for that reason he
chose to let him have me, though he could sell me to
his own brother-in-law for a great deal more money
than what he got from this gentleman. Mr King, my
new master, then made a reply, and said the reason he
had bought me was on account of my good character;
and, as he had not the least doubt of my good behaviour, I should be very well off with him. He also
told me he did not live in the West Indies, but at
Philadelphia, where he was going soon; and, as I understood something of the rules of arithmetic, when we
got there he would put me to school, and fit me for a
clerk. This conversation relieved my mind a little and
I left those gentlemen considerably more at ease in
myself than when I came to them; and I was very
thankful to Captain Doran, and even to my old master,

for the character they had given me; a character which I afterwards found of infinite service to me. I went on board again, and took my leave of all my shipmates; and the next day the ship sailed. When she weighed anchor I went to the waterside and looked at her with a very wishful and aching heart, and followed her with my eyes until she was totally out of sight. I was so bowed down with grief that I could not hold up my head for many months; and if my new master had not been kind to me, I believe I should have died under it at last. And indeed I soon found that he fully deserved the good character which Captain Doran had given me of him; for he possessed a most amiable disposition and temper, and was very charitable and humane. If any of his slaves behaved amiss, he did not beat or use them ill, but parted with them. This made them afraid of disobliging him; and as he treated his slaves better than any other man on the island, so he was better and more faithfully served by them in return. By this kind treatment I did at last endeavour to compose myself; and with fortitude, though moneyless, determined to face whatever fate had decreed for me. Mr King soon asked me what I could do; and at the same time said he did not mean to treat me as a common slave. I told him I knew something of seamanship, and could shave and dress hair pretty well; and I could refine wines, which I had learned on shipboard, where I had often done it; and that I could write, and understood arithmetic tolerably well as far as the Rule of Three. He then asked me if I knew any thing of gauging; and, on my answering that I did not, he said one of his clerks should teach me to gauge.

Mr King dealt in all manner of merchandize, and kept from one to six clerks. He loaded many vessels in a year; particularly to Philadelphia, where he was born, and was connected with a great mercantile house in that city. He had besides many vessels and droggers of different sizes, which used to go about the island and other places to collect rum, sugar, and other goods. I understood pulling and managing those boats very well; and this hard work, which was the first that he set me to, in the sugar seasons, used to be my constant employment. I have rowed the boat, and slaved at the oars, from one hour to sixteen in the twenty-four; during which I had fifteen pence sterling per day to live on, though sometimes only ten pence. However, this was considerably more than was allowed to other slaves that used to work often with me, and belonged to other gentlemen on the island: these poor souls had never more than nine-pence a day, and seldom more than six-pence, from their masters or owners, though they earned them three or four pisterines a day: for it is a common practice in the West Indies, for men to purchase slaves, though they have not plantations themselves, in order to let them out to planters and merchants, at so much a-piece by the day, and they give what allowance they choose out of this produce of their daily work to their slaves for subsistence; this allowance is often very scanty. My master often gave the owners of those slaves two and a half of these pieces per day, and found the poor fellows in victuals himself, because he thought their owners did not feed them well enough according to the work they did. The slaves used to like this very well, and as they knew my master to be a man of feeling, they were always glad to work for him in preference to any other gentleman; some of whom, after they had been paid for these poor people's labours, would not give them their allowance out of it. Many times have I seen these unfortunate wretches beaten for asking for their pay; and often severely flogged by their owners if they did not bring them their daily or weekly money exactly to the time; though the poor creatures were obliged to wait on the gentlemen they had worked for, sometimes more than half the day, before they could get their pay; and this generally on Sundays, when they wanted the time for themselves. In particular, I knew a countryman of mine, who once did not bring the weekly money directly that it was earned; and though he brought it the same day to his master, yet he was staked to the ground for his pretended negligence, and was just going to receive a hundred lashes, but for a gentleman who begged him off fifty. This poor man was very industrious, and by his frugality had saved so much money, by working on shipboard, that he had got a white man to buy him a boat, unknown to his master. Some time after he had this little estate, the governor wanted a boat to bring his sugar from different parts of the island; and, knowing this to be a negro-man's boat, he seized upon it for himself, and would not pay the owner a farthing. The man on this went to his master, and complained to him of this act of the governor; but the only satisfaction he received was to be damned very heartily by his master, who asked him how dared any of his negroes to have a boat. If the justly-merited ruin of the governor's fortune could be any gratification to the poor man he had thus robbed, he was not without consolation. Extortion and rapine are poor providers; and some time after this, the governor died in the King's Bench, in England, as I was told, in great poverty. The last war favoured this poor negro-man, and he found some means to escape from his Christian master; he came to England where I saw him afterwards several times. Such treatment as this often drives these miserable wretches to despair, and they run away from their masters at the hazard of their lives. Many of them in this place, unable to get their pay when they have earned it, and fearing to be flogged as usual, if they return home without it, run away where they can for shelter, and a reward is often offered to bring them in dead or alive. My master used sometimes in these cases, to agree with their owners, and to settle with them himself; and thereby he saved many of them a flogging.

Once, for a few days, I was let out to fit a vessel, and I had no victuals allowed me by either party; at last I told my master of this treatment, and he took me away from him. In many of the estates, on the different islands where I used to be sent for rum or sugar, they would not deliver it to me, or to any other negro; he was therefore obliged to send a white man along with me to those places; and then he used to pay him from six to ten pisterines a day. From being thus employed, during the time I served Mr King, in going about the different estates on the island, I had all the opportunity I could wish for, to see the dreadful usage of the poor men; usage that reconciled me to my situation, and made me bless God for the hands into which I had fallen.

I had the good fortune to please my master in every department in which he employed me; and there was scarcely any part of his business, or household affairs, in which I was not occasionally engaged. I often supplied the place of a clerk, in receiving and delivering cargoes to the ships, in tending stores, and delivering goods; and, besides this, I used to shave and dress my master when convenient, and take care of his horse; and when it was necessary, which was very often, I worked likewise on board of different vessels of his. By these means I became very useful to my master, and saved him, as he used to acknowledge, above a hundred pounds a year. Nor did he scruple to say I was of more advantage to him than any of his clerks; though their usual wages in the West Indies are from sixty to a hundred pounds current a year.

I have sometimes heard it asserted, that a negro cannot earn his master the first cost; but nothing can be further from the truth. I suppose nine tenths of the mechanics throughout the West Indies are negro slaves; and I well know the coopers among them earn two dollars a day; the carpenters the same, and oftentimes more; also the masons, smiths, and fishermen, &c. and I have known many slaves whose masters would not take a thousand pounds current for them.

But surely this assertion refutes itself; for, if it be true, why do the planters and merchants pay such a price for slaves? And, above all, why do those, who make this assertion, exclaim the most loudly against the abolition of the slave trade? So much are we blinded, and to such inconsistent arguments are they driven by mistaken interest! I grant, indeed, that slaves are sometimes, by half-feeding, half-cloathing, over-working, and stripes, reduced so low, that they are turned out as unfit for service, and left to perish in the woods, or expire on a dunghill.

My master was several times offered by different gentlemen one hundred guineas for me; but he always told them he would not sell me, to my great joy: and I used to double my diligence and care for fear of getting into the hands of those men who did not allow a valuable slave the common support of life. Many of them used to find fault with my master for feeding his slaves so well as he did; although I often went hungry, and an Englishman might think my fare very indifferent; but he used to tell them he always would do it, because the slaves thereby looked better and did more work.

While I was thus employed by my master, I was often a witness to cruelties of every kind, which were exercised on my unhappy fellow slaves. I used frequently to have different cargoes of new negroes in my care for sale; and it was almost a constant practice with our clerks, and other whites, to commit violent depredations on the chastity of the female slaves; and these I was, though with reluctance, obliged to submit to at all times, being unable to help them. When we have had some of these slaves on board my master's vessels to carry them to other islands, or to America, I have known our mates to commit these acts most shamefully, to the disgrace, not of Christians only, but of men. I have even known them gratify their brutal passion with females not ten years old and these abominations some of them practised to such scandalous excess, that one of our captains discharged the mate and others on that account. And yet in Montserrat I have seen a negro-man staked to the ground, and cut most shockingly, and then his ears cut off bit by bit, because he had been connected with a white woman who was a common prostitute: as if it were no crime in the whites to rob an innocent African girl of her virtue; but most heinous in a black man only to gratify a passion of nature, where the temptation was offered by one of a different colour, though the most abandoned woman of her species.

One Mr Drummond told me that he had sold 41,000 negroes, and that he once cut off a negro-man's leg for running away – I asked him, if the man had died in the operation? How he, as a Christian, could answer for the horrid act before God? And he told me, answering was a thing of another world; but what he thought and did were policy. I told him that the Christian doctrine taught us to do unto others as we would that others should do unto us. He then said that his scheme had the desired effect – it cured that man and some others of running away.

Another negro man was half hanged, and then

burnt, for attempting to poison a cruel overseer. Thus by repeated cruelties are the wretched first urged to despair, and then murdered, because they still retain so much of human nature about them as to wish to put an end to their misery, and retaliate on their tyrants! These overseers are indeed for the most part persons of the worst character of any denomination of men in the West Indies. Unfortunately, many humane gentlemen, by not residing on their estates, are obliged to leave the management of them in the hands of these human butchers, who cut and mangle the slaves in a shocking manner on the most trifling occasions, and altogether treat them in every respect like brutes. They pay no regard to the situation of pregnant women, nor the least attention to the lodging of the field-negroes. Their huts, which ought to be well covered, and the place dry where they take their little repose, are often open sheds, built in damp places; so that, when the poor creatures return tired from the toils of the field, they contract many disorders, from being exposed to the damp air in this uncomfortable state, while they are heated, and their pores are open. This neglect certainly conspires with many others to cause a decrease in the births as well as in the lives of the grown negroes. I can quote many instances of gentlemen who reside on their estates in the West Indies, and then the scene is quite changed; the negroes are treated with lenity and proper care, by which their lives are prolonged, and their masters are profited. To the honour of humanity, I knew several gentlemen who managed their estates in this manner; and they found that benevolence was

101

their true interest. And, among many I could mention in several of the islands, I knew one in Montserrat whose slaves looked remarkably well, and never needed any fresh supplies of negroes; and there are many other estates, especially in Barbadoes, which, from such judicious treatment, need no fresh stock of negroes at any time. I have the honour of knowing a most worthy and humane gentleman, who is a native of Barbadoes, and has estates there. This gentleman has written a treatise on the usage of his own slaves. He allows them two hours for refreshment at mid day; and many other indulgencies and comforts, particularly in their lying; and, besides this, he raises more provisions on his estate than they can destroy; so that by these attentions he saves the lives of his negroes, and keeps them healthy, and as happy as the condition of slavery can admit. I myself, as shall appear in the sequel, managed an estate, where, by those attentions, the negroes were uncommonly cheerful and healthy, and did more work by half than by the common mode of treatment they usually do. For want, therefore, of such care and attention to the poor negroes, and otherwise oppressed as they are, it is no wonder that the decrease should require 20,000 new negroes annually to fill up the vacant places of the dead.

Even in Barbadoes, notwithstanding those humane exceptions which I have mentioned, and others I am acquainted with, which justly make it quoted as a place where slaves meet with the best treatment, and need fewest recruits of any in the West Indies, yet this island requires 1000 negroes annually to keep up the original stock, which is only 80,000. So that the whole term of a negro life may be said to be there but sixteen years! and yet the climate here is in every respect the same as that from which they are taken except in being more wholesome. Do the British colonies decrease in this manner? And yet what a prodigious difference is there between an English and West India climate.

While I was in Montserrat, I knew a negro man, named Emanuel Sankey, who endeavoured to escape from his miserable bondage, by concealing himself on board of a London ship: but fate did not favour the poor oppressed man; for being discovered when the vessel was under sail, he was delivered up again to his master. This *Christian master* immediately pinned the wretch down to the ground at each wrist and ankle, and then took some sticks of sealing-wax, and lighted them, and dropped it all over his back. There was another master who was noted for cruelty, and I believe he had not a slave but what had been cut, and had pieces fairly taken out of the flesh: and after they had been punished thus, he used to make them get into a long wooden box or case he had for that purpose, in which he shut them up during pleasure. It was just about the height and breadth of a man; and the poor wretches had no room when in the case to move.

It was very common in several of the islands, particularly in St Kitt's, for the slaves to be branded with the initial letters of their master's name, and a load of heavy iron hooks hung about their necks. Indeed, on the most trifling occasions they were loaded with chains, and often other instruments of torture were added. The iron muzzle, thumb-screws, &c. are so well known, as not to need a description, and were sometimes applied for the slightest faults. I have seen a negro beaten till some of his bones were broken, for only letting a pot boil over. It is not uncommon, after a flogging, to make slaves go on their knees, and thank their owners, and pray, or rather say, God bless them. I have often asked many of the men slaves (who used to go several miles to their wives, and late in the night, after having been wearied with a hard day's labour) why they went so far for wives, and why they did not take them of their own master's negro women, and particularly those who lived together as household slaves? Their answers have ever been – 'Because when the master or mistress choose to punish the women, they make the husbands flog their own wives, and that they could not bear to do.' Is it surprising that usage like this should drive the poor creatures to despair, and make them seek a refuge in death from those evils which render their lives intoler-able – while,

> With shudd'ring horror pale, and eyes aghast,
> They view their lamentable lot, and find
> No rest

This they frequently do. A negro man on board a vessel of my master's, while I belonged to her, having been put in irons for some trifling misdemeanor, and kept in that state for some days, being weary of life, took an opportunity of jumping overboard into the sea; however, he was picked up without being drowned.

Another, whose life was also a burden to him, resolved to starve himself to death, and refused to eat any victuals: this procured him a severe flogging; and he also, on the first occasion which offered, jumped overboard at Charles Town, but was saved.

Nor is there any greater regard shewn to the little property than there is to the persons and lives of the negroes. I have already related an instance or two of particular oppression out of many which I have witnessed; but the following is frequent in all the islands. The wretched field slaves, after toiling all the day for an unfeeling owner, who gives them but little victuals, steal sometimes a few moments from rest or refreshment to gather some small portion of grass, according as their time will admit. This they commonly tie up in a parcel; either a bit's worth (six pence) or half a bit's worth; and bring it to town, or to the market, to sell. Nothing is more common than for the white people on this occasion to take the grass from them without paying for it; and not only so, but too often also to my knowledge, our clerks, and many others, at the same time, have committed acts of violence on the poor, wretched, and helpless females, whom I have seen for hours stand crying to no purpose, and get no redress or pay of any kind. Is not this one common and crying sin, enough to bring down God's judgment on the islands? He tells us, the oppressor and the oppressed are both in his hands, and if these are not the poor, the broken-hearted, the blind, the captive, the bruised, which our Saviour speaks of, who are they One of these depredators once, in St Eustatia, came on board of our vessel, and bought some fowls and pigs of me; and a whole day after his departure with the things, he returned again and wanted his money back: I refused to give it, and, not seeing my captain on board, he began the common pranks with me; and swore he would even break open my chest and take my money. I therefore expected, as my captain was absent, that he would be as good as his word; and he was just proceeding to strike me, when fortunately a British seaman on board, whose heart had not been debauched by a West India climate, interposed and prevented him. But had the cruel man struck me, I certainly should have defended myself at the hazard of my life; for what is life to a man thus oppressed? He went away, however, swearing; and threatened that whenever he caught me on shore he would shoot me, and pay for me afterwards.

The small account in which the life of a negro is held in the West Indies is so universally known, that it might seem impertinent to quote the following extract, if some people had not been hardy enough of late to assert that negroes are on the same footing in that respect as Europeans. By the 329th Act, page 125, of the Assembly of Barbadoes, it is enacted, 'That if any negro, or other slave, under punishment by his master, or his order, for running away, or any other crime or misdemeanor towards his said master, unfortunately shall suffer in life or member, no person whatsoever shall be liable to a fine; but if any man shall out of *wantonness, or only of bloody-mindedness, or cruel intention, wilfully kill a negro, or other slave, of his own, he shall pay into the public treasury fifteen pounds sterling.*'

And it is the same in most, if not all, of the West India islands. Is not this one of the many acts of the islands which call loudly for redress? And do not the assembly which enacted it, deserve the appellation of savages and brutes rather than of Christians and men? It is an act at once unmerciful, unjust, and unwise; which for cruelty would disgrace an assembly of those who are called barbarians; and for its injustice and *insanity* would shock the morality and common sense of a Samaide or a Hottentot.

Shocking as this and many other acts of the bloody West India code at first view appear, how is the iniquity of it heightened when we consider to whom it may be extended. Mr James Tobin, a zealous labourer in the vineyard of slavery, gives an account of a French planter, of his acquaintance, in the island of Martinico, who shewed him many Mulattoes working in the fields like beasts of burden; and he told Mr Tobin, these were all the produce of his own loins! And I myself have known similar instances. Pray, reader, are these sons and daughters of the French planter less his children by being begotten on black women! And what must be the virtue of those legislators, and the feelings of those fathers, who estimate the lives of their sons, however begotten, at no more than fifteen pounds, though they should be murdered, as the act says, *out of wantonness and bloody-mindedness?* But is not the slave trade entirely at war with the heart of man? And surely that which is begun, by breaking down the barriers of virtue, involves in its continuance destruction to every principle, and buries all sentiments in ruin!

I have often seen slaves, particularly those who were meagre, in different islands, put into scales and weighed, and then sold from three-pence to six-pence, or nine-pence a pound. My master, however, whose humanity was shocked at this mode, used to sell such by the lump. And at or after a sale, even those negroes born in the islands, it is not uncommon to see husbands taken from their wives, wives taken from their husbands, and children from their parents, and sent off to other islands, and wherever else their merciless lords choose; and probably never more during life see each other! Oftentimes my heart has bled at these partings; when the friends of the departed have been at the water-side, and with sighs and tears have kept their eyes fixed on the vessel till it went out of sight.

A poor Creole negro I knew well, who, after having often been thus transported from island to island, at last resided in Montserrat. This man used to tell me many melancholy tales of himself. Generally, after he had done working for his master, he used to employ his few leisure moments to go a fishing. When he had caught any fish, his master would frequently take them from him without paying him; and at other times some other white people would serve him in the same manner. One day he said to me, very movingly, 'Sometimes when a white man take away my fish, I go to my master, and he get me my right; and when my master, by strength, take away my fishes, what me must do? I can't go to any body to be righted'; then, said the poor man, looking up above, 'I must look up to God Mighty in the top for right.' This artless tale moved me much, and I could not help feeling the just cause Moses had in redressing his brother against the Egyptian. I exhorted the man to look up still to the God on the top, since there was no redress below. Though I little thought then that I myself should more than once experience such imposition, and need the same exhortation hereafter, in my own transactions in the islands; and that even this poor man and I should some time after suffer together in the same manner, as shall be related hereafter.

Nor was such usage as this confined to particular places or individuals; for, in all the different islands in which I have been (and I have visited no less than fifteen) the treatment of the slaves was nearly the same; so nearly indeed, that the history of an island, or even a plantation, with a few such exceptions as I have mentioned, might serve for a history of the whole. Such a tendency has the slave-trade to debauch men's minds, and harden them to every feeling of humanity! For I will not suppose that the dealers in slaves are born worse than other men – No! it is the fatality of this mistaken avarice, that it corrupts the milk of human kindness, and turns it into gall. And, had the pursuits of those men been different, they might have been as generous, as tender-hearted, and just, as they are unfeeling, rapacious, and cruel. Surely this traffic cannot be good, which spreads like a pestilence, and taints what it touches! Which violates that first natural right of mankind, equality and independency, and gives one man a dominion over his fellows which God could never intend! For it raises the owner to a state as far above man as it depresses the slave below it; and, with all the presumption of human pride, sets a distinction between them, immeasurable in extent, and endless in duration! Yet how mistaken is the avarice even of the planters. Are slaves more useful by being thus humbled to the condition of brutes, than they would be if suffered to enjoy the privileges of men? The freedom which diffuses health and prosperity throughout Britain answers you – No. When you make men slaves, you deprive them of half their virtue, you set them, in your own conduct, an example of fraud, rapine, and cruelty, and compel them to live with you in a state of war; and yet you complain that they are not honest or faithful! You stupify them with stripes, and think it necessary to keep them in a state of ignorance; and yet you assert that they are incapable of learning; that their minds are such a barren soil or moor, that culture would be lost on them; and that they came from a climate, where nature (though prodigal of her bounties in a degree unknown to yourselves) has left man alone scant and unfinished, and incapable of enjoying the treasures she has poured out for him! An assertion at once impious and absurd. Why do you use those instruments of torture? Are they fit to be applied by one rational being to another? And are ye not struck with shame and mortification, to see the partakers of your nature reduced so low? But, above all, are there no dangers attending this mode of treatment? Are you not hourly in dread of an insurrection? But, by changing your conduct, and treating your slaves as men;

every cause of fear would be banished. They would be faithful, honest, intelligent and vigorous; and peace, prosperity, and happiness would attend you.

THE STORY OF PENGUIN CLASSICS

Before 1946 ...'Classics' are mainly the domain of academics and students, without readable editions for everyone else. This all changes when a little-known classicist, E. V. Rieu, presents Penguin founder Allen Lane with the translation of Homer's *Odyssey* that he has been working on and reading to his wife Nelly in his spare time.

1946 *The Odyssey* becomes the first Penguin Classic published, and promptly sells three million copies. Suddenly, classic books are no longer for the privileged few.

1950s Rieu, now series editor, turns to professional writers for the best modern, readable translations, including Dorothy L. Sayers's *Inferno* and Robert Graves's *The Twelve Caesars*, which revives the salacious original.

1960s The Classics are given the distinctive black jackets that have remained a constant throughout the series's various looks. Rieu retires in 1964, hailing the Penguin Classics list as 'the greatest educative force of the 20th century'.

1970s A new generation of translators arrives to swell the Penguin Classics ranks, and the list grows to encompass more philosophy, religion, science, history and politics.

1980s The Penguin American Library joins the Classics stable, with titles such as *The Last of the Mohicans* safeguarded. Penguin Classics now offers the most comprehensive library of world literature available.

1990s The launch of Penguin Audiobooks brings the classics to a listening audience for the first time, and in 1999 the launch of the Penguin Classics website takes them online to a larger global readership than ever before.

The 21st Century Penguin Classics are rejacketed for the first time in nearly twenty years. This world famous series now consists of more than 1300 titles, making the widest range of the best books ever written available to millions – and constantly redefining the meaning of what makes a 'classic'.

The Odyssey continues ...

The best books ever written

PENGUIN CLASSICS

SINCE 1946

Find out more at www.penguinclassics.com